CONSIDERING
CHILDREN

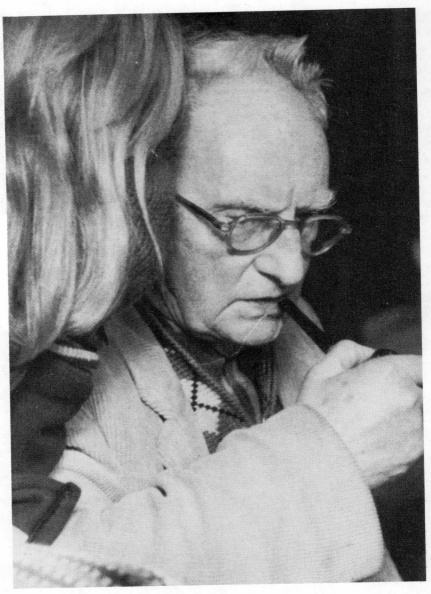

A.S. Neill, founder of Summerhill, made a point of listening to pupils with unfeigned concentration. He believed that the best way to have a healthy influence on children is to be on their side, whatever they do.

CONSIDERING
CHILDREN

DAVID GRIBBLE

DORLING KINDERSLEY

Considering Children was edited and designed by
Dorling Kindersley Limited, 9 Henrietta Street, London WC2E 8PS

Editor Donald Berwick
Designer Peter Luff

First published in Great Britain in 1985 by
Dorling Kindersley Limited

British Library Cataloguing in Publication Data

Gribble, David
  Considering children.
  1. Education of children
  I. Title
  370   LB880.G6/
  ISBN 0–86318–081–7
  ISBN 0–86318–082–5 Pbk

Typeset by Cambrian Typesetters, Frimley, Surrey
Printed by Billings in Great Britain

After a traditional education at Eton and Cambridge and three years as a teacher at Repton, David Gribble joined the staff at Dartington Hall School, where he at last made contact with what he describes as 'the only honest system of education'. Both he and his wife teach at Dartington, and all four Gribble children were educated at the school. After 11 years as head of first the Junior, then the Middle School, he is now coordinating a new programme that gives Senior and Middle School children fresh opportunities to design their own curricula.

David Gribble's spare-time activities are broad and varied. While at Cambridge, where he read Modern Languages, he wrote material for the Footlights and edited *Granta* for a year. He has published a Christmas play and a set of songs and has written the words and music for several musicals that have been performed by amateur groups. A jazz enthusiast, he plays the piano, tenor sax, double bass and guitar. And he has contributed crossword puzzles to *The Listener*, the peak of the crossword-setters' Parnassus. Above all, though, he concentrates his time and energy on giving young people the best possible chance to build a happy future not only for themselves but also for the world they will inherit.

'. . . in every serious idea born in anyone's brain, there is something that cannot possibly be conveyed to others, though you wrote volumes about it and spent thirty-five years in explaining your idea; something will always be left that obstinately refuses to emerge from your head and that will remain with you for ever; and you will die without having conveyed to anyone what is perhaps the most vital part of your idea.'

(from *The Idiot*,
by Feodor Dostoievsky)

Contents

Contents

Preface

Taking a long view, the progressives have had an astonishing success in the last half-century. A.S. Neill of Summerhill and W.B. Curry of Dartington wanted all schools to become like theirs, coeducational. That is largely what has happened. They wanted corporal punishment to be banned generally as it was by them. Although there is still progress to be made, it now looks as though it will not be long before Britain falls into line with the rest of Europe and the archaic sticks, belts and taws which have been used for so long to hit Britain's children with are put away in their last resting places. They wanted children for symbolic reasons to wear clothes which children chose rather than having them chosen by adults, and at least uniforms are no longer so uniform or so universal. Above all, they wanted children to be treated with no less respect just because they were children, and in this too they have succeeded beyond the wildest hopes they harboured when they first began to put their doctrines into practice.

But taking a short view, the progressives have been forced into tight-lipped caution. We are now living through a period of reaction. Ascendant are the educational conservatives who want not just to stand pat but to go back to the 19th century when children were kept in their proper place, neither heard nor seen. For a short time it has been the conservatives who speak with confidence. The progressives, reformers and idealists, though not silenced, have taken to whispering. They need to have more courage.

This is why David Gribble's book is so refreshing. After half a lifetime of teaching at Dartington he has sprung to the defence of progressive education at a time when it has been under

9

severe attack, and has drawn on all the experience he has gained to indicate the principles which underlie the practice at his school and at similar ones elsewhere.

He at least has not been affected by the mood of any black papers. He is as enthusiastic and as forthright as the pioneers were in their heyday, so much so that his book is as much a classic as the original statements made by Neill and Curry. It has that ring to it, not just because on occasion he uses the same sort of language as they did – 'The Case Against Original Sin' is vintage stuff – but because he does so well what they did: let the children speak for themselves. The 13-year-old girl is the true voice of Dartington and of many other schools when Gribble quotes the commandments she developed for herself:

> Love your work.
> Never let yourself down.
> Help anyone who needs it.
> Enjoy yourself, but don't hurt other people while you do.

The words and photographs of many progressively educated children and Gribble's skill combine to show what a school can be like when it is not overwhelmed by routine, even in these days when public examinations cannot be ignored. He evokes the bubbling enthusiasm for life which all young children have when, in Traherne's words,

> The corn was orient and immortal wheat, which never should be reaped, nor was ever sown. I thought it had stood from everlasting to everlasting.

The vivacity and vividness of children need not be tamed by any school system. It can be encouraged in an atmosphere in which adults and children are able to learn together.

Michael Young
President, Advisory Centre for Education

Introduction

For twenty years I have been trying to explain the idea of progressive education. I have tried my hand at articles for magazines, prospectuses, advertisements and philosophic notes for staff and parents. I have talked, written letters and replied to criticisms from adults. I have discussed issues with children over and over again, individually, in classes, in small groups. Never have I been able to convey the whole of what I believe to be the only morally justifiable method of educating children.

So now I have written a book.

Some people visiting a progressive school for the first time seem to recognise all at once an ideal they have long dreamed of. Others take time to appreciate it. A few never understand its merits at all. Reactions to this book will probably be similar. It is intended to encourage the dreamers and to help persuade the doubters. Inveterate opponents it will only irritate.

In times of economic anxiety these inveterate opponents become active, and progressive education is threatened, particularly in the state sector. Teachers are expected to produce scientists and to train school-leavers for jobs, not to mess about with independence of thought or individual preferences. This makes my book all the more timely, as I find myself putting forward the view that even in terms of producing good workers and high-flying academics, progressive methods work better than conventional ones.

To produce good workers is not the primary purpose of progressive education; it is a useful by-product. I hope that by the end of my book the primary purpose, abstract and elusive though it may be, will have become a little clearer and will be seen to justify the methods used to achieve it, hitherto so often maligned and misunderstood.

Most of my professional career has been spent at Dartington Hall School, which has recently had more than its fair share of being maligned and misunderstood; but this book is not intended to be a justification of any particular school, and I make no reference in my main text to Dartington's highly publicised troubles in 1983 and 1984. I refer anybody who wishes to read about them to my postscript entitled 'The anti-progressive bias of the press' (p. 183).

Other schools have embarrassing administrative problems, and at other schools there are, alas, sometimes tragic accidents, but the media do not generally imply that a conventional school is itself responsible for such troubles when they occur; the headlines are reserved for progressive schools like Dartington Hall. Such treatment does a disservice to education.

I believe in what Dartington Hall is trying to achieve, and I am a loyal member of the staff. Its name turns up frequently in the following pages. The arguments in *Considering Children*, however, are entirely my own. I have not attempted to describe Dartington Hall School itself, and my views do not necessarily coincide with those of my colleagues.

How I came to progressive education

'He had been eight years at a public school, and had learnt, so I understood, to make Latin Verses of several sorts, in the most admirable manner. But I never heard that it had been anybody's business to find out what his natural bent was, or where his failings lay, or to adapt any kind of knowledge to him. He had been adapted to the verses, and had learnt the art of making them to such perfection, that if he had remained at school until he was of age, I suppose he could only have gone on making them, over and over again, unless he had enlarged his education by forgetting how to do it. Still, although I had no doubt that they were very beautiful, and very imposing, and very sufficient for a great many purposes in life, and always remembered through life, I did doubt whether Richard would not have profited by someone studying him a little, instead of him studying them quite so much.'

(From Bleak House, *by Charles Dickens)*

At a simple level progressive education can be seen merely as a reaction against the mistakes of conventional education. That was how I started myself, when, after a comparatively liberal time at Eton and Cambridge, I began my teaching career in a typical public school. An account of my reactions against my experiences there may prove a helpful introduction to the complex and subtle subject matter of my book.

Repton is a school near Derby, in the middle of England and in the middle of the public-school tradition. I taught languages there for three years in the 1950s, immediately after leaving

Cambridge. I took up teaching because I liked children and it seemed a socially useful thing to be doing. State schools would only take trained or experienced teachers, and as I wanted to start work at once, I had to go to an independent school which was satisfied with a degree.

At first I enjoyed my work. It was sometimes disagreeable – for instance when I had difficulty with my classes – but I liked the boys, I ran a jazz-band, a play-reading society and the school magazine, and my memories of my time there are mainly pleasant. However, as time passed I became dissatisfied.

My first doubts were about the values of the school.

Games were paramount and were regarded as a training more in loyalty than in physical health and skill. During my first term a sixth-former was beaten because he had chosen to work in the laboratory rather than to watch a school football match. All the boys had to watch school football matches, and while they were being played academic work was not merely less important, it was forbidden.

As I knew from my own experience at school, the humiliation of an official beating is as important as the actual pain inflicted. To be forced to accept a beating is to abandon one's body to another person in a way that no child should ever be asked to do. You have to accept that your body, and indeed your mind, are someone else's to command, or else you must either cultivate an unnatural indifference or rebel. None of these courses is desirable.

While I was teaching at the school a boy was killed playing cricket. He was hit on the head by the ball when playing at silly mid-on. At the end of the term the headmaster gave a talk in the chapel, and he said what a sad term it had been – because the wife of one of the older teachers had died; the boy's death was hardly mentioned. Few of the boys even knew what the dead woman had looked like. For the headmaster adults mattered more than children, and it apparently did not occur to him that his pupils might feel differently. Accidents in sport had to be taken as part of the game.

I had to stop watching school football matches myself because I could not take the implications of heroism when an injured player was cheered as he limped back on the pitch. If he was really injured, in other words if it was true heroism, it was heroism in a false cause. The cheering showed how successful the school was at creating an atmosphere of fanatical loyalty; and this was not loyalty to a person or loyalty to an ideal, it was loyalty to an institution. If there was any ideal involved, it was the ideal of loyalty as a virtue in itself – an ideal dear only to totalitarians.

One non-conforming boy who played the violin used to annoy his fellow-pupils by saying 'The Queen is an ass.' When he did so they took him to the bathroom and threw him in a cold bath with his clothes on. This clever political argument did not convince him, and I imagine he is still antiroyalist today. All he could have learnt was a hatred and fear of the crowd who hold accepted opinions. Nevertheless, the story was told among the staff with an amused tolerance.

ORDERS FROM ABOVE

Another issue that bothered me was hierarchy. Not only was the headmaster inaccessible, but even the housemasters were aloof from the younger staff. One day while we were waiting in the lodge for the boys to walk past to the classrooms, one of the housemasters knocked a ruler off the marshall's table. As he began to stoop to pick it up he noticed me standing nearby, and so he waited. At first I was so annoyed that I did nothing, but then I picked it up for him. This trifling incident stood for a great deal; if he behaved in this way with a fellow member of staff, how on earth did he behave with the boys? There is a natural consideration due to age or infirmity, and everyone is owed a certain courteous helpfulness, but to demand respectful servility from others is a poor example to set. As many ex-public-school people demonstrate, it is an example that is readily followed.

I expect I was a nuisance. I was even foolish enough to criticise the headmaster, and I almost lost my job. It was all about a poem that had been submitted for the school magazine and had been set up for printing when the headmaster saw it. The poem, called 'Repton', was only mildly disillusioned with the school; its most outspoken line was 'Repton, Repton, Repton, repetition.' The headmaster called the poet to his study and gave him a stern dressing-down. I heard about this and sent a note saying that I had been responsible for letting the poem through and I thought he really should have been seeing me. Then it was my turn. I was sent for to the headmaster's study – the only time I had been there since my original interview. I still remember his exact words: 'If you think you can tell me how to run the school, then the sooner you start looking for another job the better.'

This incident, too, with its censorship, its Olympianism and its unfairness, both to me and to the boy, taught me more than at first appears on the surface. Autocracy may be an effective way of getting things done, but it is useless as a method of education. If you want to change someone's opinion – and education is largely a matter of developing people's opinions – you cannot do so by threats. Opinions are developed by experience and discussion. What the poet and I learned from that experience was that our views were not considered worth discussing, and that in future we ought to keep our heads down. Perhaps those were indeed the lessons the headmaster intended us to learn. They are lessons which, if properly learnt, would be likely to prevent any true education of the mind.

LACK OF MUTUAL TRUST

My dissatisfaction with the school deepened as I came to understand the level of mistrust between adults and children. I find it easy to get on with adolescents, and they usually like me, but at Repton I could count the friends I made among the boys on the fingers of one hand. There was no chance of being accepted as a friend and an equal in the Grubber after school, although some of the staff sometimes went there; the friends I made were boys who played jazz with me, or read plays, or edited the magazine. In the end some of them might even drop in to see me uninvited, but the occasions were rare. The unwanted aura of respect clung round me in spite of the fact that I was only a few years older than my pupils.

The near impossibility of a close social relationship disappointed me because I enjoyed the company of young people. The age difference, anyway, was small. During my first year a distant relation was a pupil at the school, and to meet him and talk to him in a normal way was a great refreshment. 'Normal' is perhaps the key word in that sentence; the relationship between adults and children was stilted, artificially respectful or condescending, and it was the painful and abnormal lack of any real contact that I found so uncongenial.

SEXUAL SEGREGATION

Another abnormality in the situation was the absence of the opposite sex. Even the staff met almost no unattached women. The idea that this enforced celibacy would produce a decorous innocence was hopelessly wrong. Where there are no girls to attract them, boys are attracted by other boys, and any 13-year-old with smooth cheeks and long eyelashes becomes aware of the effect he has on others. How far this goes depends mainly on the older boys concerned; the head of one of the houses at Eton when I was there claimed to have been in bed with every boy in the house. Staff, too, with no feminine acquaintance, are attracted by the fluttering eyelashes, and you often see a sort of flirtatious teasing between a master and a pretty youth.

All this, though, is probably not the worst result of an all-male school. The worst result is the attitude of the boys to girls. A public-school education might have been designed to teach boys to regard girls as sex-objects, because that is the only light in which they make contact with them. Boys only meet girls at parties. There is no chance of working together, of chatting in the school yard, of appreciating each other as people; there is only the convention-laden school dance, or the deafening disco where conversation is impossible. The girls are even dressed up seductively for the occasion. Add to this the boys' occasional obscene conversation and the pin-ups they cut out of magazines, and it is a wonder that a public-school man ever manages to form a genuine relationship with a woman.

When I was teaching at Repton I was reduced to blushing embarrassment by the mere presence of any woman between 12 and 40. A visit to the cinema with one would have been gossip for the rest of the young staff for weeks. If a school can have this effect on a 25-year-old who has, after all, lived a normal life among both sexes for some time, imagine the effect it may have on a 15-year-old who has never had a sensible conversation with any woman except his mother.

My decision to leave Repton came when I accidentally had a boy caned for me. When people are expected to act contrary to their own convictions they often make clumsy blunders, and this was one of mine. There was a rule that boys were not allowed to eat sweets in class. Unfortunately a boy in my class not only ate some sweets, which I might have managed not to notice, but threw one across the classroom to a friend.

Your reaction to this crime probably depends on whether you are a teacher or not. A non-teacher might well see it as an act of generosity, and not particularly disturbing to the class. A traditionally trained schoolmaster sees it as an act of deliberate disobedience which must be instantly punished. I accordingly felt I must set the poor child some lines. Lines had to be written on special blue paper which could only be obtained from housemasters. The boy went to his housemaster and asked for the paper, and was asked why he was being punished. He told all, and as the standard punishment for eating in class was a caning, the housemaster caned him.

After this I realised that I could not go on teaching in a school whose philosophy was so different from my own. Without having another job I handed in my notice.

THE SCENE CHANGES

At about this time I read a book by Victor Bonham-Carter about Dartington Hall, with a section on the school by Bill Curry, the headmaster who had built it up. It seemed to hold the answers to all my problems, and I wrote to ask whether there was a place for me. The German teacher had had to leave unexpectedly, and so, in the summer term just before I left Repton, Hu and Lois Child, Curry's successors, invited me down for an interview.

The contrast was so great that during the interview I gained very little idea of what the school was truly like. My principal impression was one of colour. After months of grey herring-bone the brightness of the Dartington children's clothes was astonishing. A beautiful girl came up to me and asked me, extremely pleasantly, what I was doing there, if that wasn't a rude question. (No Repton boy could have acted so naturally.) My interview in the study with Hu and Lois was interrupted by a barefoot girl who burst in, dripping blood on the floor, to ask for help as she had cut her foot on a piece of glass. (The head's study at Repton was a protected shrine.) One of the teachers

Schools can enforce uniformity of clothing, but not of personality. Children are more likely to be happy and self-confident, and to develop a sense of values of their own, when allowed to wear what they like.

who interviewed me wore shorts. Dazed and confused, I accepted the job I was offered, and so began my discovery of what seems to me to be the only possible honest system of education.

Repton was not sorry to see me go. One of the senior staff told me that L.K. Elmhirst, the founder of Dartington, was an old Reptonian. 'Not a very good one, I'm afraid,' he said. In the school magazine the next term there was a short list of the staff who had left, most of them to be headmasters of other schools. I was at the end: '. . . and Mr Gribble, who has gone to lend a hand at a co-educational school in the south of England.'

My first half-term holiday I spent visiting Repton with the jazz musician Lionel Grigson, who was then a pupil at Dartington. When we returned Hu and Lois asked us to give a joint talk about Repton to any children who were interested, and L.K. Elmhirst came to listen. When we had finished he told us why he was not considered a good old Reptonian. In the boarding houses there, five or six boys, one from each age group, had to share studies, and the youngest one or two were fags. There was no escape, and there was much opportunity for bullying. When Repton launched an appeal for money, L.K. said he would contribute only if the study system were changed. He did not have to contribute.

This change Repton did not make. It does now take a few girls, as do many other public schools, and even a few girls must make a great difference. However, I hope that much of what I have said will be sufficiently familiar for you to feel that there is still something fundamentally wrong with the conventional approach to education. I have seen plenty of children come to Dartington as educational casualties in the '70s and '80s, some from schools with bad or sadistic teachers, many others from schools where most of the pupils made satisfactory progress and were reasonably contented. At Dartington the children's attitudes to school have usually changed within a few weeks – sometimes in as little as one day – and after their attitudes have changed they have begun to learn again.

Perhaps there are few schools left where grown-ups hit children, but there can be no doubt that most schools are still intolerant, insensitive and unsympathetic places. Many of them, particularly independent ones, still make no effort to adapt the work to the child, but simply attempt to adapt the child to the work. The work may no longer be Latin verses, but the criticisms are still the same as those in Dickens's *Bleak House*, quoted at the beginning of this chapter.

I have known intelligent and industrious children who had to be dragged or even carried into the traditional sort of school – often a reputable and generally successful one. What can it have done to make sensitive and conscientious children hate it so much? What may it still be doing to children who are tough enough to take the atmosphere, but cannot fail to be influenced by it?

The essence of progressive education: mutual respect

Almost anyone who visits a progressive school will notice the excellent relationship between pupils and staff and the friendly self-confidence of the children. How is this achieved? The answer is that not only do the pupils have respect for the staff, but the staff have an equal respect for their pupils. Mutual respect is at the very heart of progressive education.

Manners were invented as a form of self-defence. They were for the defence of the refined against the boorish. In the relations between grown-ups and children, however, they have too often become offensive weapons as well, with good manners usually a one-way business. It is the children who have to abandon their games to say goodbye to their parents' visitors, the children who have to open doors for teachers, the children who must never contradict. With many adults even the words 'please' and 'thank you' become condescending or facetious when used towards children. It is the children who have to stand up when a visitor comes into the room, the children who have to remain at table until everyone has finished, the children who have to sit in the back seat of the car.

I grant that all such behaviour can be pleasant and attractive. My point is that there is no expectation that the adults will be equally pleasant to the children. Parents do not have to interrupt their game of cards to say goodbye to their children's friends, teachers do not have to open doors for children, adults may contradict children whenever they like. A child who says 'please' or 'thank you' with humorous overtones or sarcastic insincerity is likely to be told off. Adults do not generally stand up when children come into the room, or stay at table until the children have finished, or take a back seat so that a child can sit in the front. When an adult does any of these things it is not thought of as good manners, it is thought of as kindness.

The headmaster of Repton when I was there apparently counted the junior staff as children. On one occasion in the school yard he told a young teacher, 'Take your hands out of your pockets when you speak to me.' This perfectly illustrates the double standard. He was allowed to be rude to the young man, but the young man was not allowed to show even the mildest sign of disrespect.

When adults are deliberately well-mannered towards children, as they are in a truly progressive school, the children are complimented, and as long as it is intended seriously, they will react seriously. When someone joins a group and courteously greets the children as well as the grown-ups, the children's pleasure is self-evident. A teacher who says 'May I see your book, please?' and who means the 'please' and is really asking a question and not giving a command, creates a feeling of good-will never achieved by the man who says 'Right, where's your book?' It means something important that if you call me David I can also call you by your first name, even if we are both adults; if one of us is a child it means still more.

A new teacher at Dartington once complained furiously to Tony Barnes, the gentlemanly head of the Middle School, that a girl had called her a bitch. 'Oh, did she?' said Tony mildly. 'What had you done to make her do that?'

The teacher's assumption had been that the children should not call her names under any circumstances. Barnes's assumption was that any child who called her a rude name must have been provoked.

ONE-WAY RUDENESS

Unfortunately the code of conventional manners makes no demands at all on the behaviour of adults towards children. It is acceptable to interrupt, to domineer, abuse, shout and even to snatch, shove and slap. I once heard, through a thick classroom wall in a comprehensive school, a maths teacher shouting, 'No, blockhead! Seven sevens are 49, not 42!' Few parents can have brought up small children without occasionally snatching dirty or precious or dangerous objects from them. But why should anyone slap a child – as I have sometimes seen happen– in an attempt, oddly enough, to stop it from crying?

Consider the following list of comparatively mild utterances commonly made by teachers – utterances that would be construed as offensive if used by a child to an adult:

'Stop fidgeting.'
'Why are you late?'
'Bring that book up here.'
'What's the matter now?'
(Interrupting) 'May I finish what I'm saying, *please*?'
'What's this supposed to be? A maths prep?'
'Sit up straight.'
'Go and wash your face.'
'Don't you speak to me like that.'

We are so used to this kind of behaviour that the strength of some of these remarks only becomes evident when we imagine a scene in which the child is making them. What will Mrs Taylor's reaction be when Cynthia, in the front row, suddenly says, 'Mrs Taylor, go and wash your face'? Mr Jones can get away with holding up Peter's untidy work for everyone to see and saying, 'What's this supposed to be? A maths prep?', but the general response will be very different if Peter holds up one of Mr Jones's badly duplicated work-sheets and asks the same question.

What this all indicates is that we broadly accept that teachers and children must be expected to be hostile to one another, and that it is necessary for teachers to humiliate children in order to retain control. They have to present themselves as superior beings who are not to be irritated by childish failings which nevertheless continually intrude on them. In order to retain their superiority they are prepared to use disdain, mockery, sarcasm, threats, personal abuse or in some cases physical violence. These are people who have chosen to become teachers, one hopes, because they are interested in children rather than in power. They must have resorted to these unattractive methods because they felt there was no other way – in fact, because they were afraid that if they did not dominate the children, the children would dominate them. In the atmosphere of hostility created by such an approach they are probably right. One teacher I knew was told during her course of teacher-training: 'You must remember, it's either you or them.'

If adults are frightened of children and use such methods to keep them down, it is clear that children will also be frightened of adults. This has more serious implications at some ages than others, and is probably most serious in the very early school years and in mid-adolescence, when the children's uncertainty as to whether they are to be treated and to react as adults or as children makes them particularly vulnerable. This latter age is precisely the age that teachers find most difficult to handle. So the problem is exacerbated and the young people have to develop either a thick skin or a group identity to protect themselves. The teachers then have to work harder to make their authority felt, and it becomes a vicious circle.

Whatever views people may hold about deliberate rudeness on the part of some teachers, everyone will agree that the most successful teachers do not need to resort to it. Whether it is that they succeed because they are polite, or only that they are able to be polite because they are successful, is perhaps still open to argument.

Pleasant manners are desirable in children as well as adults, but an authoritarian way of teaching them seems unlikely to give more than a superficial gloss. Adults who are careful with their hellos and goodbyes and thank-yous, who don't interrupt and who include children who are present in whatever is going on are more likely to teach good manners than those who are intent only on maintaining their own superiority. Adults who are domineering and offensive may keep children in order, but they will teach them nothing more valuable than how to keep their heads down and protect themselves, and by imitation the children will learn the art of abuse.

FALSE vs. TRUE COURTESY

The proper relationship between an adult and a child goes much further than conventional manners. A truly polite man, for instance, must be genuinely considerate of anyone he is talking to. It is not enough to use formulae. Formula conversation is like a duplicated letter; it contains all the right words but none of the right sentiments. In formula conversation you ask questions when you are not in the least interested in the answers: 'How are you, Mrs Harris? Had a good holiday? How are the boys getting on?' Yet if you really wanted to know the answers the questions would become compliments, and Mrs Harris might take real pleasure in answering. It is one thing to ask a question because you know it is polite, and quite another to ask the same question because you want to know the answer.

The questions people ask children are only too often examples of 'formula' politeness: 'What did you get for Christmas? And how's school going?' To ask such questions and not really listen to the answers is a typical example of adult bad manners. Every child is different. The question 'And how's school going?' has no intrinsic interest at all; it is the variety of the possible replies that is interesting, and each different reply can and should lead to a different and absorbing conversation.

In order to conduct an enjoyable conversation with anyone you have to be predisposed to listen sympathetically to what they have to say. For instance, in talking to an adult who is ignorant about some field in which you are comparatively expert, you take care not to make the other person feel foolish. Yet an extraordinary number of adults are totally insensitive about exposing children's foolishnesses; they will mock them with uninhibited delight, and even parents will often recount their own children's blunders in their presence.

Dora Russell, writing about the school she started with her husband, Bertrand Russell, at Beacon Hill, says: 'One of the most important things in the rearing of children would seem to be to prevent and to counteract their fears. They are so easily afraid – of adult displeasure, of doing or saying the wrong thing, of the dark, of failing to do things, of not being able to stand up to social contacts.' It is the second fear – that of doing or saying the wrong thing – that we are inclined to be cruelly insensitive about. When children make mistakes of this kind they are usually rebuked or laughed at immediately and in public. Not for them the prescribed behaviour in adult circles: tactful conversation after the event when you try to make light of a mistake that has been made while simultaneously giving advice about the proper way to behave next time.

THE NEED FOR CONSIDERATION
In a classroom it is often difficult to avoid humiliating an occasional student, but some teachers apparently take delight in doing so. They fail to understand that children feel humiliated only because they want to succeed, and a teacher

chokes off a powerful positive incentive by making them feel they are foolish to have tried. People who teach in adult-education classes often go to enormous lengths to make their students feel at ease, to encourage them when they have done badly, to minimise their failures and praise their achievements. Why should we think it necessary to be so much more careful of adults than of children? It is surely the children who are weaker, less experienced, more malleable, more vulnerable.

I think of myself as a considerate teacher of children and I make a good effort to avoid humiliating anyone in my classes, but when for a few weeks I had to teach German to a group of adults of very mixed ability, I found myself grovelling with apologies if anyone made a mistake, offering to set preps only if anyone wanted to do them and talking far too much myself to save the others from the embarrassment of making fools of themselves. This was of course going too far. But why was I so much more careful of the feelings of adults – who should, after all, be old enough to look after themselves – than I am of the feelings of my young pupils?

To be a valued companion it is obviously not enough to avoid humiliating children. You must also avoid imposing yourself upon them. This is true for children of all ages. I was reminded of it vividly, some time ago, by a lady who ran a very successful nursery school. In speaking of a 3-year-old boy who seemed unhappy and sat at a table by himself, not joining in with any of the other children's play, she said, 'I went over and sat beside him and tried to strike up a conversation.'

She did not go over to give the boy something to do, or to urge him to join in, or to make him tell her what the matter was. She did not go with any clear idea of what he should be doing or how she should be helping him to do it. She did not even go to strike up a conversation. She went to *try* to strike up a conversation.

This sense of social equality between adults and children is one of the essences of the progressive ideal. To some people it comes naturally, but to others it can appear to be an abdication of all dignity, all power, all adulthood. Such people will see teachers at a progressive school talking to children, and will see a wonderful relationship between pupils and teachers, but they will not easily understand how it is achieved. When you see yourself as socially superior because you are an adult, you

cannot understand that another adult may not so much set that superiority aside as actually fail to recognise its existence.

So what happens when the right kind of person tries to strike up a conversation with a child? Exactly the same as when the right kind of person tries to strike up a conversation with an adult. Anyone who talks without listening is likely to be a bore, and anyone who has decided how the conversation is to go before it starts is likely to be infuriating. Yet these are two common ways of talking to children. The secret is to listen, and to be interested, and to be open to the child's point of view as you would be to a grown-up's.

When you are talking to young children the subject may only be a game with toys, but unless you are willing to participate on exactly the same terms as you would in an adult conversation, you will fail to achieve the sense of companionship that is so desirable and so possible.

THE IMPORTANCE OF RESPECT

Courtesy and consideration, then, are two steps towards the right relationship. The third, and most important, is respect. Respect is often required by adults as if it were a one-way process: 'I am superior to you, so you treat me with respect and stand up when I come into the room and take your hands out of your pockets when I'm speaking to you!' In fact it ought always to be mutual.

Children learn what to respect by seeing what is respected. If older people do not respect them, how can they learn self-respect?

In his book *The Child's Conception of the World* Jean Piaget, the famous Swiss child psychologist, quotes a dialogue with a child that illustrates this idea in curious isolation. The child is 6 years old. He is the one who is answering all the questions:

'When you go out for a walk, what does the sun do?'
'It comes with me.'
'And when you go home?'

General acceptance of social equality between teacher and pupils – in this case during a geography lesson – is essential to the progressive ideal.

CHAPTER TWO

'It goes with someone else.'
'In the same direction as before?'
'Or in the opposite direction.'
'Can it go in any direction?'
'Yes.'
'And when two people go in opposite directions?'
'There are lots of suns.'
'Have you seen the suns?'
'Yes, the more I walk and the more I see, the more there are.'

In this interview the child's opinion is sought with apparent sincerity, and the child is never corrected. The interviewer does not ask 'What do you think the sun does?' but 'What does the sun do?' Everything the child says is written down and treated with respect. The child therefore thinks carefully, and produces sincere answers even to questions that must seem quite fat-headed to older children. It is difficult to put forward your ideas seriously to other people unless you know they are going to be taken seriously. If you become used to expecting your ideas to be ridiculed or corrected, you begin to lose faith in yourself and come to believe that the only way to be right is to borrow ideas from other people. You may even come to accept the idea that your own views are usually wrong. This is indeed a common consequence of conventional education.

The Piagettian interview that I have quoted is a good example of showing respect for a child, but it does not exemplify a valuable educational approach. The interviewer makes no positive contributions, but only asks question after question after question. In the ideal dialogue with a child you can show respect for his opinions and at the same time express your own. If you were actually talking to the boy in the interview quoted, you could quite fairly say that you didn't think there were lots of suns because you had never seen more than one at a time. A very young child might easily claim to have seen several, and then you would have either to accept the argument with some surprise, or to discuss the rarity of the phenomenon.

Even though handicapped by lack of experience and technique, most children are serious and sensible thinkers. It would be insulting to believe otherwise. It is equally insulting not to believe that they are honest and idealistic. What's more, if a boy is never believed, there is no need for him to tell the truth; if, whatever she has done, a girl is thought to have done it for motives of selfishness or idleness, she will lose confidence in her own generosity and determination. Just as a child who is treated as a fool will behave like a fool, so a child who is expected to be devious will learn to be devious. It is not only polite to anticipate high motives rather than low motives, it is also politic.

'WE FLOURISH ON APPRECIATION'

'Cram us with praise,' says Hermione in *The Winter's Tale* 'and make us fat as tame things.'

Someone I know once remarked that this expresses the whole philosophy of progressive education. It is a wise teacher who praises what is good in a child's work rather than merely correcting what is wrong. We all flourish on appreciation, and only the strongest or the most insensitive manage not to wither in its absence. We also strive to please those who appreciate us, but are unconcerned about offending those who don't. We will make no effort at all to please those who denigrate us. It follows that children obviously try harder for teachers who praise them. They must not be flattered; they must be honestly admired. It is for those who admire us that we are most willing to prove ourselves admirable.

Of course no teacher can spend her whole time honestly admiring every one of her pupils. Sometimes what they do will simply not be worthy of admiration. At such times ordinary good manners are the right course. Bad work or sulky behaviour does not put a child beneath consideration. It would be regarded as offensive to insult or abuse an adult in such circumstances; it seems to me even more offensive to insult or to abuse a child. It is possible to disagree with another person without being rude; it is possible to criticise what a person has done without being critical of the person. We used to be told to hate the sin and love the sinner; in the same way a successful teacher corrects mistakes but always lets the children know that, whatever they do, they are respected and liked.

That is the kind of trust that children need from their teachers. It is the kind of trust that once prevailed at a notable – but now, alas, defunct – London comprehensive school, Risinghill (of which I shall have much more to say in the next chapter). Michael Duane, the head of Risinghill, simply accepted his pupils' behaviour when they swore at him, when they stole, when they ran away from home, and he went on talking to them just as he had talked to them before. In the end, as he spoke reasonably to them, so they responded reasonably; as he treated them with respect, so they respected him.

An experimental educational programme at The Terrace in Conisbrough, Yorkshire, a few years ago took on fifteen 15-year-old boys from Northcliffe Comprehensive School who seemed unlikely to gain any benefit at all from conventional lessons and were causing problems for other pupils by their anti-social behaviour. At The Terrace they were encouraged to take part in discussions, and they found that their opinions were valued and they were able to make decisions about how their work was to be organised. The adults were there to help, but the boys were in charge.

Of course there was more to the scheme than this. The boys' time was mainly spent on practical work, for which they earned money, though to begin with this was done with the slack indifference with which they had approached ordinary school work. But it seems to me likely that it was the elements of courtesy, consideration, respect and praise for work well done that caused the great change in their attitude. By the end of a year they were generally considered to be alert, self-confident and sensitive, and a group of teachers asked to assess their intelligence rated them all as average or above average.

Paradoxically enough, if you *compel* a child to be polite you inhibit any feeling of goodwill. If you *organise* class 3B to do community work on Tuesday afternoons you are likely to find them reluctant. If you *demand* a child's respect you may only succeed in making yourself disliked. Goodwill, consideration and genuine respect cannot be forced; they grow only when children have been allowed to acquire a proper confidence in themselves.

The ideal progressive teacher makes no requirements of the children in terms of personal behaviour towards herself. As a result the children treat her with affection and loyalty. In all dealings between her and the children, she listens to what they have to say. When they see that they are listened to, they come to understand that what they think is important. When they understand that what they think is important, they begin to think seriously about important matters. By thinking seriously about important matters they come to important conclusions.

It is not only right to treat children with respect, it is also expedient. That is why you will notice the friendliness of both pupils and staff at a progressive school if you visit one.

History as a stalking-horse

I am not yet ready to launch into a full discussion of what I see as the basic attitudes that distinguish proper from improper educational aims. I shall approach that discussion cautiously, using other people's ideas and experiences as stalking-horses.

Let me start with Rousseau's *Emile*, a novel in which the great French thinker expounded his ideas about the best way to educate children. There is much that Rousseau got wrong back in 1762, but what he got right is enough to point the way to the approach I am going to describe – and to show that many of the ideas underlying progressive education are by no means new. Rousseau is in fact often termed the 'father' of progressive education.

Emile is a fictitious account of the education of a young aristocrat, brought up by a tutor in what Rousseau considered to be the ideal way. In spite of the irrelevance of this style of education today, and in spite of many alarmingly authoritarian opinions, much of what Rousseau said is still valid, and in 1762 must have been astonishing.

EMILE'S CURRICULUM

Rousseau wanted Emile to learn only what he – the child – could appreciate as useful. In 1762 the notion that children should learn only what *they* could appreciate as useful must have seemed an abdication of the educator's responsibility. It was the educator who had to tell children what they should learn, and what the children thought of it no one cared. The question of usefulness was quite irrelevant; an educated man was not necessarily a useful man at all, he was just someone who had at one time learnt Latin and Greek and Ancient History.

Rousseau's views were extreme. He did not expect a child to appreciate the advantages of learning to read, and he therefore devised a cunning scheme for persuading the child to want to learn to read for his own ends. This was to arrange for him to receive a series of written invitations to enjoyable events. The child would sometimes be able to find someone to read them to him, but at other times he would have to puzzle them out for himself, so that he would soon be begging for instruction.

It seems unlikely that a child would learn to read a book merely from the study of invitations, however frequently they came, but the scheme shows vividly Rousseau's determination that the child should see a purpose in all that he learnt. Just before he expounds this system he mentions other people's efforts to find good reading methods, and then exclaims, 'What a pity! A better means than any of these, and one which is always forgotten, is the desire to learn. Give the child this desire, and then forget about your desks and your dice; any method will work.'

Most of Emile's education was to be practical. He was to live in the country and to become a gardener and a carpenter. Gardening and carpentry are clearly useful in the simplest sense, so that any child can appreciate their usefulness. The idea calls up a tremendously attractive picture of a little lad digging his plot, and watering his seeds, and picking and eating his fruit, at the same time learning about the seasons and manure and pollination and pests, and sawing and hammering away at wood, making wonderful chairs and tables and learning the value of accuracy, and how to measure, and the properties of different woods, and how to make a stable structure, and the necessity for perseverance. (What this picture leaves out is the fact that for most children most of the time gardening and carpentry are much too slow, and most of the work is in itself extremely boring to a child. The endearing picture of the child learning from his practical activities is possible only when he is really interested in what he is doing, and to interest a child in gardening requires as much skill as to interest him in Latin.)

Nowadays most people would agree that a child should learn what is useful. There is indeed a worrying tendency to think that a child should *only* learn what is useful, and ignore literature, music, art, morals and philosophy. However, the *child's* opinion as to the usefulness of the knowledge he is to acquire is still generally regarded as irrelevant.

What is more, in spite of the general agreement about children learning what is useful, in practice they seldom do. The examination system becomes the chief motivating force, and what is examined is often not intended to be of practical use to the child who is being examined. How many people who passed O-Level physics or maths now make any use of their knowledge, apart from the most elementary information about electricity or arithmetic? It may well be important for some other reason to understand coefficients of friction or to have learnt to solve quadratic equations, but it is certainly not useful, in the narrow sense, to more than a very small proportion of the people who have learnt about such things.

As long as examinations remain the only door to interesting jobs and further education, schools will have to go on teaching children to pass them, and children will accept the drudgery for the sake of the long-term aim. Good teachers will manage to interest and even inspire their pupils in spite of the system, not because of it.

And as long as examinations remain in their present form it will be impossible to teach only what is useful, because the amount of knowledge that can be taught in school, and that is genuinely useful to every possible individual, is so small. Arithmetic is usually quoted as essential, but how often does an ordinary person need to multiply by more than two or three? There is much stress nowadays on the importance of studying sciences, but who uses scientific knowledge except the scientists? A farmer does not base his use of fertilizers on what he learnt in O-Level biology; he bases it on what he learnt as a farmer about fertilizers.

A core curriculum, if it were to be limited to what was genuinely useful to everybody, would consist of reading, writing and simple manipulation of measurements and quan-

Rousseau was right to believe that children enjoy making things and that they learn as they do so.

tities. What has to be added to this is not more of what is useful, but more of what is interesting.

On the question of curriculum, then, Rousseau is still a step ahead, even of the modern educators who think children should only learn what is useful. He says children should learn what *they can appreciate* as useful; the difference in what is learnt may be small but the difference in the approach to the child is enormously significant.

ENJOYMENT OF LESSONS

Rousseau also wanted Emile to enjoy his instruction. This seems such a self-evident advantage to people who are not school-teachers that it is difficult to see why the idea is not universally accepted. Even Dr. Johnson said, 'What is learnt without inclination is soon forgotten.'

There are various ways of trying to make a child enjoy lessons. The feeblest way is to suggest that no child need do anything that doesn't immediately attract him. This leads to a gloomy aimlessness, and to the joke about the child who said, 'Please, miss, do I have to do whatever I like again today?' Achievement is a pleasure, and learning is a pleasure, but they have to be worked for. What is needed is not so much superficial enjoyment, which is often short-lived, but a sense of purpose and an understanding of the enjoyment to be found by following a purpose through.

The public-school way is to fill your lessons with idio-syncrasies and jokes. There was a French teacher during my time at Eton who, whenever he saw a chain hanging from a boy's pocket – we used to fasten penknives to them – would cry out, 'Ha! A chain! Penalty for improper use, five pounds.' He also quoted Kipling – 'The class laughed subserviently' – and we laughed subserviently, and we laughed because it was funny, and we enjoyed our lessons very much. I can remember more of his jokes, and I can remember the way he used to smile and look up at the corner of the ceiling when he made a joke; I cannot, alas, remember anything at all about his teaching of French.

It is an advantage to the conventional teacher if his lessons are popular, because the children are more amenable and his work is therefore easier. However, in the teacher's eyes at least, the main objective is that his pupils should acquire some

particular knowledge and not that they should enjoy themselves. There is no chance of abandoning some topic and
turning to another because a particular class is not interested;
the examination system prevents it. John Holt, a modern
American writer on education, has suggested that, instead of
deciding what their classes ought to know and teaching them
about that, teachers should find something that their classes
are stimulated by and teach them about that. Unfortunately
this idea is still alien to most of us 200 years after Rousseau
wrote his book.

SELF-RELIANCE

Another of Rousseau's objectives was that Emile should learn
to rely on his own judgement and experience. In three key
sentences he rejects three of the basic duties of the conventional teacher:

'The tutor must not lay down precepts, he must let them
be discovered.'
'Don't let [Emile] learn science, let him invent it.'
'To substitute books [for personal experience] does not
teach us to reason; it teaches us to use other people's
reasoning; it teaches us to believe a great deal but never to
know anything.'

Convention holds that teachers must lay down rules of
behaviour, and teach information, and insist on children
learning from books. How else will they learn how to behave,
or know any facts, or have any opinions? In the above three
sentences, two of them remarkably short, Rousseau gives the
alternatives.

Where precepts are concerned, he saw that morality was not
an artificial code invented by the upper classes for their own
protection, but a natural state of affairs that even a child could
find out for himself. This is one of the major leaps still required
of any parent who is going to send a child to a progressive
school. Most people still feel that unless you instruct children
about right and wrong, there is no way in which they can learn.
This point of view was expressed to me bluntly by one of the
masters at Repton. During a discussion with other staff I had
said that I did not think children needed rules to tell them what

was right and wrong. In desperation the master exclaimed, 'But if you don't tell them, how are they ever going to know?'

Put briefly, the progressive answer is that moral laws are implicit in the need of human beings to live together. I shall expand on this later in this book.

Inventing science rather than learning it – to discuss Rousseau's second sentence – is becoming a common approach in the early stages, although the invention is inclined to be so structured with pre-planned 'experiments' and carefully chosen equipment that there is little chance of genuine exploration. So much of modern scientific knowledge is quite remote from everyday life that a student without careful guidance is not likely to get far. Here again, for most children, the issue is one of interest rather than usefulness.

On books, of course, Rousseau overstates his case. If everything could be learnt by personal observation it would have been unnecessary for him to write *Emile*. He was attacking a system of education which depended entirely on books, a system which persisted into the twentieth century. He wanted the authority of books questioned, and the information they gave to be tested against personal experience.

Emile was not to accept what he read or was taught without questioning it. In terms of conventional education he was to be a rebel. In conventional terms, teacher knows best, and it is the teacher's duty to pass on what he knows to the child, and to insist on the child learning it thoroughly. Emile was not to be brought up to accept that kind of instruction.

Many teachers still cannot accept the right of the child to question what is taught. We had a very clear example at Dartington: a woman who taught, of all uncontroversial subjects, P.E. She did not much enjoy working with us and left and took a job at the local comprehensive. She much preferred it, and a friend asked why. 'The children don't ask so many questions,' she said.

Rousseau himself believed the tutor to be vastly superior to Emile, but the tutor was nevertheless to train Emile in independence of thought. There seems to be something paradoxical about the idea of using one's authority over another person to train that person in independence, but Rousseau believed it to be possible. In his view this freedom of thought was certain to lead to Emile sharing his opinions, because the natural truth was bound to be revealed to anyone who sought it independently and without preconceptions.

A rather less arrogant version of this belief seems to me fundamental to the progressive ideal, as I shall explain in a later chapter.

CHILDREN, NOT ADULTS

Rousseau was also ahead of his time in wanting children to remain children for as long as possible; he did not want them to be, as his century required, merely inexperienced grown-ups. 'Childhood has its own ways of seeing, thinking and feeling,' he says, and 'They [teachers] are always looking for the man in the child, without thinking what he is before he becomes a man.'

He understood and enjoyed aspects of childhood that most people disapprove of. In explaining away a small child's destructiveness, he says, 'Making things is always slow, and . . . destroying them, because it is faster, suits his vivacity better.' In discussing justice he comments:

'The first feeling for justice does not come from that which is due to others, but from that which is due to us.'

Rousseau manages to make this statement without moral disapproval; a feeling for justice is a good thing, to whomever the justice is due, and it is from the childish demands for fairness that a general idea of justice grows.

In one of the most enjoyable passages in the whole book he demolishes La Fontaine as a suitable author for children. Taking the fable of the crow, the fox and the cheese, he analyses it line by line from a rational child's standpoint. The first line is *'Maître corbeau, sur un arbre perché,'* and this is what Rousseau has to say:

'Maître! que signifie ce mot en lui-même? que signifie-t-il au-devant d'un nom propre? quel sens a-t-il dans cette occasion?

Qu'est-ce qu'un corbeau?

Qu'est-ce qu'*un arbre perché*? L'on ne dit pas *sur un arbre perché*, l'on dit *perché sur un arbre.*'

His final observation is that no children will learn the correct lesson from the fable anyway. They will not identify with the foolish crow so as to realise that flattery is deceptive; they will identify with the cunning fox, and will learn that flattery can be rewarding.

This exercise in seeing things from the child's point of view is carried out several times in the book, yet it is still something that most grown-ups, including teachers, find almost impossible to do.

Society is still astonishingly frightened of its young. Until young people are restrained by the necessity of holding down a job or caring for a family, they are thought of as irresponsible and dangerous. Commercial interests cater for them and provide them with a huge range of toys, books, magazines, motor-bikes, electronic games and pop music. Educators, on the other hand, try to draw them as fast as possible into the world of adult convention, the world of 'Semi-Detached, Suburban Mr Jones' as Manfred Mann put it. 'What a poor sort of foresight,' wrote Rousseau, 'to make a child wretched in the present with the more or less doubtful hope of making him happy at some future day.' It seems as apt a comment as ever.

To recapitulate, Rousseau wanted Emile to learn only what he could appreciate as useful, to enjoy his instruction, to learn to rely on his own judgement and experience, and to remain a child for as long as possible.

These are the kinds of opinion people refer to when they describe him as the father of progressive education.

WHERE ROUSSEAU FAILS

In some ways, the ideas set forth in *Emile* are far from progressive. For one thing, Rousseau assumes that the tutor always knows best, and his duty is to guide the child into the proper channels by any means that occur to him, including force, bribery and deception. It would be difficult to imagine an approach further from what I see as the progressive ideal.

'Use force with children, and reason with men,' wrote Rousseau. And later on: 'Up to this age [about 17] it was necessary to constrain [Emile] or deceive him in order to have him obey you.' He wanted every child to be a devout believer in whatever was the religion of his own country. Emile was to be quiet, resigned, docile and obedient – hardly the type of child one expects to find in a progressive school. So that he could be protected from evil influences he was to be educated alone, out in the country, and his tutor was to supervise him all day and all night.

Rousseau's views on the education of women can be summed up in one quotation:

'Thus we see that all education of women must be relative to men. To please them, to be useful to them, to win their love and respect, to bring them up when they are young, to care for them when they are grown, to advise them, console them and render their lives agreeable and sweet; those are the duties of women at all times, and those are what they should be taught from early childhood.'

How can a man who held such views as these possibly be regarded as the father of progressive education? The answer is that he was halfway there.

THE 1934 *MODERN SCHOOLS HANDBOOK*

In our own century and our own country, feelings about conventional education similar to mine had already inspired reform before I was born. Optimism about new approaches was voiced in the 1934 *Modern Schools Handbook*, which was published at a time when independent progressive schools were flourishing and many parents were becoming excited about the new ideas. The handbook, to which all the first great progressive heads contributed, was intended to help people choose the right school for their children. It covered 21 schools, and included descriptions of what were then the seven main co-educational progressive schools in Great Britain: Beacon Hill, Bedales, Dartington Hall, Frensham Heights, King Alfred, St. Christopher and Summerhill.

The book is very much less high-flown than Rousseau, and much of it is dull; factual descriptions of school facilities could hardly be otherwise. Even in the interesting parts the heads tend to criticise conventional practice rather than frankly stating their educational philosophies as Rousseau does. Their criticisms are precise and well-argued, however, and because they are criticisms of the type of education most of us received, they bring general progressive ideas into a clearer focus.

For Rousseau the enemy was society, the antithesis of natural virtue; nowadays this seems somewhat paranoid. For the first progressive heads in 20th-century Britain the enemies were other schools, in particular the public schools. Although this is still to miss the point, because the argument is really about something much deeper, at least the target was worth attacking, and the attack itself implied many of the values that motivated it.

'A school is something more than a place for learning second-hand knowledge of the past,' wrote Badley of Bedales, 'and its activities are not to be confined to imitation of old models and to games, with a cadet corps as its training for citizenship and a First or a Blue at the university as a final goal of ambition.'

I do not suppose that any modern public school would accept this description of itself, but learning second-hand knowledge is still the central part of almost every curriculum, and though the cadet corps may be out of fashion, athletic success and above all a university place are still the major targets. Development of other sides of the personality is much less important.

THE MENACE OF COMPULSION

'It is often found,' said Roberts, of Frensham Heights, 'that children coming from schools where games are compulsory wish to avoid them.' This theme was echoed time and again. Compulsion is not a good way of developing a child's interest and enthusiasm, even in a subject as popular as sport. In other subjects it is clearly counter-productive. Curry, of Dartington Hall, put the same point like this: 'It is sometimes maintained that it is good for children to study subjects they dislike. This view seems to confuse learning a subject with attending classes in it.'

Neill, the founder of Summerhill, was even more precise about the effects of authoritarian teaching: 'Gertrude, aged 13, arrives from a convent. At the convent she has learned to hate all lessons, has never had to show any initiative, has never had to think for herself.'

Few schools intend to prevent children from thinking for themselves, fewer wish to prevent initiative, and none intend to induce hatred of learning. Nevertheless, many still do so.

Curry, in giving his reasons for abandoning competitive marking, offered also a partial explanation for the lack of enthusiasm for learning among school children:

'At the same time we [at Dartington] find ourselves departing, for purely educational reasons, from the tradition that marks and competition are necessary in order to secure an adequate standard of effort and industry. First because experience shows that, while it undoubtedly encourages some of the children, it is apt to discourage those who most need encouragement, and it does not therefore succeed in its professed object; secondly because, by directing the attention of both teacher and pupil to those aspects of the subject-matter which can be marked, it is apt to direct the attention away from those aspects which are most significant; and thirdly because, by relying upon motives which are extraneous to the subject-matter in hand, it fails to provide a basis for any enduring interest in the study itself.'

It is in part the search for the enduring interest, the discussion of the most significant aspects of the subject-matter and the desire to encourage those who most need encouraging that still distinguish the progressive approach. In this sense all the best teachers must surely be progressive, but they are often forced to act within a framework of marks and competition that sadly inhibits them.

Doubts about the value of religious instruction were also extremely important to a number of the 1934 heads, though not all. Curry explained his position like this: 'In the modern world, dogmatic religious instruction provides a very unstable basis for morality, since after the experience of the last generation we must suppose that a large proportion of those who are taught dogmatic religion in childhood will cease to believe it when they grow up.'

It is important to notice that he did not question the value of moral education, but only the effectiveness of religious instruction as a means of bringing it about. He was not suggesting that, in losing their religion, the parents of 1934 had also lost all sense of moral values. A sounder approach than religious education would be the education of the emotions; but Curry was sceptical about the possibility of any such education in a single-sex community, where 'everything is done to make emotional experience as difficult as possible to come by, and as unnatural as possible when it occurs.'

CHAPTER THREE

A 'BARBARIC CODE'

What disturbed all these heads was the effect, as they saw it, of conventional education. The results that everyone hoped for – wise, moral, just and learned citizens – were the exception rather than the rule. A. S. Neill, of Summerhill, saw this as a direct consequence of the disciplinary system in schools:

'Because schools have been opposed to the real interests of the child, we have had to compel the child to adapt himself by imposing upon him a barbaric code of reward and punishment, thereby introducing the child to fear and deceit and hate. The system was linked to the belief that the child is born evil and must be made good by some external adult authority.'

It seems clear that a child who is not introduced to fear, deceit and hate by a system of reward and punishment must already have some strong moral values. If you have no moral values, you will cheat to gain rewards as long as you are not prevented from doing so by the fear of punishment. A child, therefore, must be good before coming into contact with the system if the system is to have the desired effect. And if the child is already good, the system, being anyway unpleasant, is also unnecessary, and should therefore be jettisoned.

Neill did not limit the evil effects of discipline to the individual. 'We have had disciplined schools for a long time in Europe,' he wrote, 'and they do not seem to have led us anywhere in particular. Today, Europe is an armed camp ready for war.'

Remember that this was written in 1934.

Discipline is often closely associated with aggression. Royston Lambert's research into boarding-school education, described in his book *The Hothouse Society* (published by Weidenfeld & Nicholson in 1968), showed that in schools where the staff are violent the pupils are likely to be violent too. Europe is still an armed camp.

In spite of the attack led by those who wrote the 1934 *Modern Schools Handbook*, conventional British education has gone happily on, providing instruction in subjects children dislike, driving them on by a spirit of competition and reinforcing fear and deceit with reward and punishment. Half a century after 1934, many schools still separate boys and girls, attach neurotic importance to games and, by implication, prepare their pupils for war. Britain remains the only European country which allows adults to beat children with sticks.

RISINGHILL

Finally, listen to the true story of an amazing school in Islington, London, where for a short time 20 years ago a man named Michael Duane put progressive principles into action and showed that progressive education is not just an expensive luxury for the privileged classes. As the head of Risinghill Comprehensive School for the whole of its brief life from 1960 to 1965, Duane began by being ready to accept the conventions of the state-school system, but with the intention of making gradual improvements as he saw the opportunity. First, since school uniforms and holding the door open for 'Sir' seemed totally out of character in Islington, he gave up insisting on these customs. He then set up a school council where the majority of members were children, and he kept an open study door for any children or parents who wanted to see him at any time. He encouraged discussion, and when a member of his teaching staff complained about a child he listened to the child's side of the story too. Most important of all, he was able to abolish corporal punishment.

To do this in Islington, then one of the toughest areas in London, with children who were used to being hit by their parents as well as their teachers, showed extraordinary conviction. To do so with a number of teachers appointed to his staff who disapproved of his approach was dedication to the point of rashness; tragically, in spite of a huge reduction in the number of children on probation, improving examination results and press headlines like 'WILD SCHOOL IS TAMED BY LOVE', the Inner London Education Authority closed the school just as it was beginning to flourish. Parents protested furiously, and children wept, but Risinghill, with all it represented to the people of Islington, was simply obliterated.

Its tough inner-city location was not Risinghill's only disadvantage. A quarter of the children were foreign, and many did not even understand English adequately. The school was formed from two secondary moderns and two technical schools; three of these had been single-sex. Rivalry among them had been encouraged, and all of them believed in firm

47

HANDS OF RISINGHILL School

MR DUANE MUST STAY

DOWNING ST.

discipline and control. Two of the former heads, philosophically opposed to Michael Duane, were appointed to the staff before he was selected himself.

It was in the face of all these problems that a staff meeting decided to do without corporal punishment, and Michael Duane, surprised and delighted, announced the decision to the children.

ORDER OUT OF CHAOS

Anyone who has taught at a progressive school knows what it is like when a child comes in from a repressive background. At Risinghill they had to cope with this situation in an extreme form. Michael Duane described the problem and its eventual solution in an interview with Elspeth Huxley which first appeared in *Punch*. 'You go through a period of sheer chaos with each incoming batch,' he told her. 'The children don't believe there's no cane. They have to test your statement. They shout and yell and make life impossible. You have to stand there and let them call you all the four-letter words and every obscenity in the language. You've got to go on talking and whatever happens keep your temper. It's a nightmare for the teachers and some of them can't take it. I don't blame them. But it's the only way.

'When the children grasp the fact that there really *isn't* any

Michael Duane put progressive principles into action when he was head of Risinghill Comprehensive School. He lasted only 5 years – from 1960 to 1965, when, in spite of children's tears and parents' protests, the Inner London Education Authority firmly closed the school. The I.L.E.A. never again employed Michael Duane as a head, although he applied for many headships. During his time at Risinghill he encouraged discussion, kept an open study door, abolished corporal punishment and established a cordial relationship with a student body whose examination results improved steadily throughout the five years.

cane they calm down. In any case they get tired of chaos eventually and then you can start to talk to them like reasonable human beings. It works in the end.'

'It seemed to,' commented Elspeth Huxley after visiting Risinghill. 'At any rate the school was orderly – the children appeared to be usefully employed and not carving up each other or the staff.'

In fact by the time the school had been running 18 months the children who were used to the atmosphere took care of the newcomers themselves, and there was no more chaos.

'It's the only way,' Michael Duane said. It was the only way to show these children that at Risinghill they really would be treated with a respect they had never met anywhere else, that here they would truly find a refuge from the violence outside. These children lived in a world where crime, drunkenness and prostitution were commonplace, yet when they finally realised that they were being treated as reasonable human beings it was as reasonable human beings that they reacted.

In such a background Michael Duane's first objective was to teach these unrespected children a proper self-respect, to help them see that their opinions counted, that they were important as individuals. When a reporter asked him, towards the end of the life of the school, 'What are you really aiming at here?' he answered: 'To remove fear from children in schools.'

In spite of the support of a number of fine teachers, with the staff he had he could not go as far as he would have liked. The children regarded him as a friend, but they called him 'Sir'. There was no official corporal punishment, but there *was* punishment; he himself had no time for it, but the school continued to have detention and the giving of report and attendance cards. Individual teachers still clouted children.

The attitudes of the world outside were as much in need of change as the attitudes of the worst of his teachers. 'If our society,' he said at prize day in 1963, 'were to give up the hypocritical pretence that this is a Christian country actuated by Christian principles when the difference between the wealthy and the poor is so blatant, and were to bend its efforts towards making Christian love or basic democracy a reality, then there would be no limit to the progress we could achieve with our children.'

The inspectors who visited the school in 1962 did not think

highly of Christian love and basic democracy as practised at Risinghill. Michael Duane 'esteems cordiality among the major virtues,' they said scornfully, and 'Sometimes in avoiding terror the school has abandoned awe.'

Cordiality, which means warmth of heart and sincerity, might perhaps be thought of by many as an aspect of Christian love, and therefore among the major virtues. To teach children to feel awe before perfectly ordinary men and women is surely to deceive them. Cordiality and the absence of awe seem to me to be highly admirable. They are the hallmarks of a progressive school.

In 1965 Risinghill, orderly and racially harmonious in spite of its astonishingly difficult setting, was simply shut down – closed, allegedly, to make room for a general reorganization. However, the I.L.E.A. has never employed Michael Duane again, though he applied for several headships. It seems inexplicable when you consider the following statistics:

1. Examination Results

	O-Level Candidates	Number who passed at least one*	A-Level Candidates	University Entrants
1960	18	5	0	0
1961	32	16	0	0
1962	39	20	0	0
1963	59	34	0	0
1964	80	42	3	2

* The average number of exams passed was between 3 and 4 for all these students.

2. Children on Probation
1960   98
1964   9

Risinghill, as a comprehensive school, should have had *one-fifth* of its pupils from each of five ability ranges. In fact, because of competition from two neighbouring grammar schools and six other nearby schools with better reputations in the eyes of those with academic ambitions, it never had as many as *one per cent* of its children in the top range! As the O-Level exam is designed to test only the children in that top range, fewer than two children in any one year-group at Risinghill should, statistically, have passed it.

The figures I have quoted are exactly the kind that you would expect conservative opinion to value. They are not unsupportable assertions about the children's happiness, parental approval or racial harmony. They are a demonstration that progressive methods are successful even in the most conventional terms.

They also show that progressive methods are successful with less promising children, and they may even suggest that they are most successful with the least promising children. Able and secure children will do well almost anywhere; the less able and the insecure need all the support that progressive education can give them.

After five years' work Michael Duane was deposed in spite of the fact that his methods were working. Prejudice triumphed over evidence. But though the I.L.E.A. were able to get rid of him as a headmaster, they were not able to eradicate his achievement. Opponents of progressive education sometimes argue that it may possibly work with well-motivated middle-class children, but that it is quite inappropriate for children from less privileged and less supportive backgrounds. Risinghill decisively proved the contrary.

A SUMMING UP

I have not attempted anything approaching a history of the progressive movement in this chapter. John Locke, from whom Rousseau took many of his ideas, has not been mentioned. Nor has Homer Lane, who inspired both Neill and Curry. Nor has Friedrich Froebel, who probably had a greater civilising effect on the education of young children than anyone I have mentioned. The reason for all such omissions is that my book is not a history; it is an exposition of an idea.

I have used Rousseau, the 1934 handbook and the work of Michael Duane to bring me closer to my own convictions about the true aims of education and the best ways of achieving them. Risinghill is particularly important to the argument that follows because it shows that though my experience of progressive education has been almost entirely in independent schools, the philosophy is not irrelevant to the country's entire educational system. The tragic story of Risinghill also implies a major justification for the continued existence of private progressive schools which claim to be interested in promoting a just society. Such schools are able to continue with their progressive methods in spite of the general climate of opinion or governmental pressure. The I.L.E.A. required Michael Duane to reintroduce the cane, and he refused. St. Christopher and Summerhill survive; Risinghill is history.

Summerhill survives in spite of being the most extreme of British progressive schools and having had the most provocative headmaster. It is to A.S. Neill and his extraordinary school that I shall look in the next chapter for a discussion of the limits it is unreasonable to transgress.

Freedom, not licence

Summerhill, A.S. Neill's school near Aldeburgh, was founded in the 1930s and is still running. Since his death it has been managed by his wife, and it is soon to be taken over by his daughter. Under Neill's headship it had the reputation of being the absolute in permissiveness, and Neill, who loved shocking people, rejoiced in this reputation and nurtured it in his many books and articles about the school.

Actually the reputation was not quite justified. Self-government was an important part of Neill's philosophy, and the children's own governing body at Summerhill used punishment to reinforce its decisions.

By his pretence that anything was permitted, Neill may well have done the progressive movement more harm than good. The subtle but extremely important point that he failed to emphasise was that although *he* might permit anything, the *children* did not. In this chapter I shall be mainly concerned with expanding this point in relation to progressive education generally. First, though, let me look at some of Neill's methods.

From the very beginning, the general impression of Summer-

Summerhill has suffered the reputation of being 'the absolute in permissiveness' ever since A.S. Neill founded the school more than half a century ago. This photograph shows two Summerhill children enjoying the freedom to find a quiet place for study and to make use of it.

hill among outsiders was that Neill's pupils smoked, swore, broke windows and never went to lessons. The result of going to the school was to become rude, dirty, delinquent and ignorant. It is extraordinary that anyone can have believed that a man would deliberately conduct a school with such objectives in view, but certainly in many people's eyes Neill was not simply misguided, he was wicked.

He was against corporal punishment, he was against compulsory lessons, he was against uniforms, he was against compulsory games, he was against competition, he was against authority, he was against shame; there seemed to be nothing of education left. He claimed to have high ideals; what he said he wanted above all was that children should be happy, and he wrote, 'The only possible way in education is the way of love.' A few people believed that he was an idealist and considered his views sympathetically; most decided he was wicked and refused to listen.

FREEDOM OF CHOICE

Neill believed that children who were genuinely free to choose would choose wisely. There is a dietician who says that if, every day, you offered a child a tableful of every possible kind of food from crisps and Angel Delight to whole-meal bread and beans, the child would choose a balanced diet. I do not believe that anyone has actually conducted the experiment, which would be rather expensive if conducted on a proper scale. Neill tried wholeheartedly to conduct a similar experiment in the world of education. His menu was limited – you could do fairly conventional lessons or you could play – but the choice was genuine.

He believed that any child leaving Summerhill who wanted more academic qualifications would easily be able to work for them and win them, and indeed he could tell of many such successes. If a child did not want academic qualifications it was a waste of energy to try for them; Neill also told of children who left Summerhill unqualified and nevertheless led happy adult lives.

Of course Summerhill attracted children who had failed in ordinary education, or who had other social problems. Neill's original approach to such children was Freudian. Most problems, he thought, were caused by guilt over masturbation, and indeed he actually wrote: 'The question of masturbation is supreme in education.' Since ignorance about sex apparently caused problems, he was eager to enlighten the ignorant. 'Where do babies come from?' he would ask a child clutching a doll, and receive some hostile response, but later the child would return and ask him the same question. Such conversations were called 'private lessons', but Neill eventually gave them up because he found that the atmosphere of Summerhill was therapeutic in itself.

'ON THE CHILDREN'S SIDE'

Some of his methods with difficult children were unconventional to the point of being astonishing. He would pay a child for wetting her bed, or would co-operate with a thief in a larder-raid. When he was painting a garage door and a boy came up and threw mud at it, Neill threw mud at it too.

Pause for a moment and imagine yourself in the position of any of these children. Suppose you are throwing mud at a newly painted garage door, and the man who has painted it catches you at it, and instead of tearing you apart simply joins in the game. It at once becomes clear that Neill's antics could transform children's attitudes to their own behaviour. He proved that it was possible to be on the children's side, whatever they did, and so lifted off great loads of guilt and hostility.

He loved to dumbfound children by showing them that he knew what they had done but did not disapprove. He tells of one boy who cheated him out of a pound or two by ringing up, pretending to be his own father, and asking Neill to give him money for train fare. When he found out what had happened, instead of asking for the money back, Neill went to the boy and gave him more. He told him his father had rung up to say that the fare was higher than he had realised.

This was not the only method of control in the school, however. There was also the school meeting, chaired by a child, which was the usual medium of justice. The meeting settled disputes, made rules and dealt out punishments, which were usually fines or extra work about the house and grounds. The staff were just as much subject to the results of the meeting as the children, and they had equal votes.

The idea of self-government has always been an important

one in progressive education, but one of the drawbacks is that if everything is going well, children are not particularly interested in governing. They wish to govern only if by doing so they can set right wrongs. Neill once had to declare himself a dictator with the slogan 'Heil Neill!', but none of the children minded until he began to be deliberately difficult.

The effect of Summerhill on a child coming in from another school 40 years ago must have been explosive. Imagine a 14-year-old boy, gawky and bad at games, used to being punished for having dirty shoes and caned for not learning his prep, never having had more than a few odd minutes during the day when he was not either being hurried to and fro, or prayed with, or taught at, or changing in and out of games kit, or chasing a ball, always under close supervision. He arrives at Summerhill in the clothes he likes to wear in the holidays, and finds no two children dressed alike. He meets girls who speak to him as if they were unaware of any difference of sex. People shout and laugh and wander around, and the grown-ups who are there are not telling people what to do, but are talking and laughing and wandering too, on absolutely equal terms with the children. On the first morning there are lessons, and he goes because he feels he ought to, but as he gets more used to the school he decides not to go to lessons. There are no organised games, but he soon finds himself joining in informal games, bicycling, chasing, climbing trees, perhaps even tennis or rounders.

Before long he notices that in fact most children do go to lessons, and he gets a bit bored mucking about doing nothing in particular on his own. He decides to give lessons a try, and is welcomed back. He goes through the stage of insulting grown-ups to see what happens, and nothing happens. Perhaps he tries insulting children, and is brought up before the school meeting and publicly reprimanded by the others. Nobody minds what he wears or doesn't wear. The immensity of the choice he is given, after the restrictions he was subjected to, is for a while more than he can grasp, but when at last he begins to understand that he is himself responsible for his own life and way of living, his whole approach to learning changes. He sees that education is not something imposed on you by apparently hostile adults, it is something that you yourself actively seek from adults who are willing to help. Even more important, he realises that social responsibility is not an adult imposition; it is a natural and sensible way to behave.

ARE CHILDREN NATURALLY 'GOOD'?

Personally I find this picture a convincing one. I believe it is what would have happened to me. To extend this belief to include all children is another matter; it involves an act of faith fundamental to the progressive ideal: Man is naturally good. Conventional education is based on the idea of original sin: The child is born wicked and must be taught to be good. Neill's system is based on the opposite idea: The child is born good and becomes wicked only if corrupted. My own position is in between, though very much closer to Neill's. I believe that the child is born amoral, but soon develops moral sensitivity unless mishandled or deprived.

Neill loved to flaunt his disrespect for conventions. But he found it necessary in the end to protect himself from the accusation that he let children do whatever they liked. The phrase he chose as an explanation of his position was 'freedom, not licence'. It is, unfortunately, an ambiguous phrase, which either suggests that there are limits to permissiveness or simply describes a social style. According to the first of these interpretations, Summerhill children could do what they liked as long as they did not intrude on the rights of others. That sounds fair and sensible, but it is the beginning of the denial of freedom. Different people define 'intruding on the rights of others' in different ways, and for plenty of us missing classes, for instance, falls within the definition. If one person falls behind in the lessons, it can be argued, all the rest of the class are held up. And so on.

In a short time all the freedoms of Summerhill could be argued away. 'Freedom, not licence' becomes a useful catch-phrase for anyone who wants to stop other people from doing what they like. And, interpreted in this way, it also implies a denial of Neill's basic assumption that a *free* child is a *responsible* child. If that assumption is right, a free child should never wish for licence.

'Freedom, not licence' as the description of a social style, however, is absolutely consistent with Neill's ideals. In simply describing the general atmosphere of a progressive school, it says that the children's behaviour is free but not licentious. I

hope this is what Neill really meant, because it seems to me to be true that licence is not a consequence of *freedom*; it is a reaction against *repression*.

RULES THAT MAKE SENSE

There must be limitations to freedom, of course, and there were plenty of rules at Neill's Summerhill. At one time all the trees in the grounds were classified as trees you were allowed to climb or trees you were not allowed to climb. If there was a thief or a bully in the school the other children had to be protected. There were fixed meal-times and bed-times. To explain all these restrictions as a ban on licence is rather far-fetched. It is hardly licentious to climb a forbidden tree. I prefer the explanation given by Tony Barnes, who was for many years head of the Middle School at Dartington: 'The point is not that there should be no rules, but that there should be no rules except ones that the children can see to be necessary.'

I met Neill only when he was old and tired, and I never visited Summerhill during the term, but I taught for two terms at Kilquhanity House, a small school in Scotland run on similar lines. Once a week I saw a school meeting in action, and I found it uninspiring. There are two attitudes to rules to be found among progressive teachers. One is that you have as few rules as possible but make sure they are kept; the other is that it doesn't matter how many rules you have, no one need pay much attention to them. Kilquhanity inclined towards the latter view. Meetings were often long wrangles about who had started the quarrel which ended in someone getting spat at, and what the punishment should be for whoever it was. Most infringements of the many rules were punished by fines, or ignored.

There was frequent public bickering, and the whole school had to sit around the edge of the dining room and listen to these depressing discussions, of absorbing interest only to the

Adolescents are at an age when one of the main purposes of life is to establish one's identity. The freedom to decorate your own room is a useful aid to this process.

participants. Very often, after a subject had been aired for some time, the pupil chairman would turn to John Aitkenhead, the headmaster, and say, 'Well, John, what do you think we ought to do?', and the meeting would accept John's opinion.

There seemed to me to be three weaknesses to these meetings: The whole school had to listen to the discussion of issues relevant to only two or three children; the decisions of the meeting were influenced by the headmaster to a point where the children were accepting his views as automatically superior to their own; and there was a traditional feeling that if something went wrong you simply made another rule about it rather than removing the cause. Half-way self-government is little more educational than autocracy.

PROBLEMS WITH SELF-GOVERNMENT

Self-government for children has always been an ideal of progressive educationists, but in practice it raises problems. The main problem is apathy on the part of the children themselves. Self-government seems like a panacea to children used to being ruled by unsympathetic adults, but to children used to a just and considerate society it seems like a chore. The pleasantest and easiest form of government is a benevolent dictatorship, and this sometimes proves to be the most attractive alternative. In order to want to govern, you have to have the wish to right wrongs, and if there are no wrongs you are particularly bothered about, why not leave things as they are?

There are two good reasons, however, why the children should take responsibility for the organization of their own society. One is educational in a narrow sense – so that they experience elections, see how democratic decisions are reached, learn how to influence them and get some idea of government from the inside. The other reason is to encourage them to see and understand that the society they live in is organised by their own representatives, for their own benefit; that rules are made by them themselves and not by adults; and that when things go wrong it is their own responsibility to put them right. This objective can only be reached if the school meeting, or council, or whatever it is called, has real authority, and even the head must obey its decisions.

If children are to have a sense that the rules are their own, the rules must continually be re-made, added to and subtracted from. Here are some extracts from the lists of rules that are now being handed out to all children at Dartington Hall Middle School at the beginning of the autumn term (These children are between 10 and 13. If nothing else, the list should demonstrate that progressive schools are not by definition schools where there are no rules. And it is not the only list. There are also bike rules, bed-time rules and swimming rules):

Rules for the easy running of the school
Among the things these rules try to do are:
— to stop children hurting themselves,
— to stop children hurting each other,
— to keep ordinary school arrangements, like lessons and Quiet Hour, running smoothly,
— to prevent damage to things, including buildings and equipment, and to help children to be happy by showing clearly what is allowed and what is not allowed.

These rules do not cover everything. That would be impossible and the list would be too boring to read properly.

General Rules
Everyone is expected to behave with care and considera-tion for others at all times. This covers everything that you do! We hope that you will try to be kind to other people but of course we can't make a rule about that.
Please listen carefully if someone does not like what you are doing.

— No smoking.
— No alcoholic drinks.

Breaking either of these rules is bad for your health, and to break the drinking rule can be extremely dangerous. We think anyone who breaks these rules may not be able to cope with the freedom in this school. Sometimes we have to tell parents, and sometimes children are sent home.
Obviously, no one may miss classes or music lessons. You must also be on time for lessons because the beginning is usually so important.

— No eating in lessons.
— It is wise to MARK OR SCRATCH YOUR NAME ON ALL
  YOUR THINGS.

Staff may make the rules they want for their own areas, including the laboratory, art room, music practice rooms, houses and gym. For instance, in the gym the rule is bare feet at all times for all children, and there is a list outside the door of the equipment you are allowed to use in free time.

If you skateboard on any ramp or do any tricks you must wear a special helmet and protective equipment.

School Council

If you do not understand any of these rules ask a house-mother, a teacher or your tutor for the reasons behind them. If you still do not think them good rules, or can suggest better ones, either come to School Council or get your class representative to put your suggestions.

The School Council is run by children, helped by a member of staff. It can discuss anything you want it to. Don't forget this school belongs to you as well as to teachers, and your opinions are very important.

If you can think of improvements, don't just grumble, don't ignore the rules as if they didn't apply to you, SPEAK OUT.

WHEN RULES ARE BROKEN

In spite of the plea at the end, these rules are seldom questioned since the young children concerned are willing to accept adult judgements most of the time. At the Senior School the tone of the rules is less paternalistic.

The question that Middle School children do ask, though, is 'Why don't you do anything about it?' when a rule is broken and nobody gets punished by adult authorities. To try to

Rules at a progressive school are not made to be blindly obeyed (or cunningly evaded); everyone in the craft block is expected to understand the reasons for these and to abide by them for the good of all.

WOODWORKERS — PLEASE READ THIS.......

1. NO PLAYING AROUND IN HERE — IT COULD BE VERY DANGEROUS

2. USE ALL EQUIPMENT AND TOOLS WITH CARE.

3. ALWAYS USE THE RIGHT TOOL FOR THE JOB THAT YOU ARE DOING. (if you don't know – ask)

4. WORK THINGS OUT CAREFULLY BEFORE YOU START MAKING SOMETHING SO THAT YOU DON'T WASTE WOOD.

5. LEARN WHERE EVERYTHING IS KEPT AND ALWAYS PUT THINGS AWAY WHEN YOUU'E FINISHED WITH THEM.

6. SWEEP UP ANY MESS THAT YOUU'E MADE ON BENCHES AND FLOOR.

I am Alice

forestall this question, the children are also given a note with the rules which starts like this:

> 'For centuries people have made animals do tricks by punishing them when they made mistakes. For centuries adults have made children do what they want by giving children punishments, even for very small things. It is different at this school. You are cleverer than animals.'

To have all this written down and given out may be a heavy-handed way of introducing children to a school, but it is probably a reassurance for many. In fact most rules are seldom invoked; there is a routine to the day that children soon fall in with, and most well-considered rules are based on either kindness or common sense.

In spite of the effectiveness of a children's council on particular disciplinary issues, the responsibility for the smooth running of a school for children under 14 still rests squarely on the adults. On the whole it is the adults who see that the rules are kept, but in doing this they are not so much policing the school as organising it in the way that the children want it organised. Even festivities are usually arranged by the grown-ups rather than the children, because the children know that they will have more fun that way.

But the adults at a happy school do not *assert* their authority. The reason a grown-up arranging a game is obeyed is not that the grown-up is a powerful figure, but that if she is not obeyed the game will be a failure. The reason children are quiet when the teacher is explaining something is that otherwise they will not hear, and will prevent others from hearing. What the grown-up stands for is in fact not authority, but an idea of rightness and justice that the children are actually keen to support.

ACCEPTABLE RESTRICTIONS

New teachers occasionally have difficulty in understanding this. Some allow every class to disintegrate into chaos because that is what the children seem to want; others, assuming that the children are hostile, shout and hector. In fact, of course, the children want their lessons to be interesting, orderly and effective, and they look to the teacher to make sure that they are so.

The right kind of situation is clearly not one in which licence prevails. It is questionable whether it can even be described as freedom. Today's progressive-school children are freer than in most other schools, but there is certainly not the absolute freedom that Neill originally seemed to champion at Summerhill. What does generally exist is a willing acceptance of necessary routine and a genuine opportunity to alter rules that seem wrong.

There can in fact be no total freedom in any society, because the mere presence of other people imposes restrictions. Even if you live alone you are not free from the need to eat and sleep, and you are not free to flap your arms and fly. What the true progressive school tries to do is, first, to create a society with as much freedom as is compatible with the *children's* objectives, and, secondly, to make sure that the *children* appreciate the reasons for the nature of the society and are free to improve or alter it if they can reach general agreement.

The key to this child-centred type of education is neither freedom nor licence, but acceptance and collective control.

For whom do schools exist?

A major reason why many people oppose progressive education is that they disapprove of the idea of a school basing its activities on a consideration of children's well-being rather than on the interests of the adult world. The term 'child-centredness' is so often used as if it were derogatory that I want in this chapter to make a serious effort to consider the alternatives.

I have managed to think of four other possible centres for education, plus one attitude that deliberately removes children from the centre without putting anything in their place and another attitude that perhaps lies behind all the rest. To these six alternatives I have given the following names: adult-centred education, society-centred education, value-centred education, group-centred education, child-suppressive education, adultism.

Out of inexperience or eagerness to please, most children accept whatever system is imposed on them. We ought to be ashamed of taking advantage of their generosity. Consider what may be imposed on them by each of the alternatives to child-centredness:

1. ADULT-CENTRED EDUCATION

Instead of considering first the needs of children, this system considers first the needs of adults. The first need of adults is to get rid of their children. They must be kept off the streets because children in the streets are almost as bad as children at home. It is impractical to put them all in prison, but you can set up special institutions called schools which will insist on children coming every day, will keep them occupied and may even teach them a few useful skills.

Dotheboys Hall, as Dickens describes it in *Nicholas Nickleby*, was an extreme example of such an institution, but as 19th-century literature shows, there used to be plenty of schools that existed primarily for this purpose.

There are still a good many adults for whom the care of their children during the daytime is a nuisance, and for whom compulsory education is a blessing of quite a different nature to that intended by idealistic educators. Boarding schools, in particular, offer months of escape for the wealthy paedophobic. This is not necessarily a bad thing, and there are plenty of affectionate and responsible parents for whom schools solve an important problem.

Another goal of adult-centred education is for the care of the children to be as undemanding as possible. There are traces of this view in the organisation of all schools; instances are staff common-rooms from which children are excluded, an insistence that children shall be punctual while teachers are allowed to be a few minutes late, official punishments for children who inconvenience staff, art only on Thursday afternoons because of the cleaners, the whole school waiting in silence while teachers take their places in assembly and an unwritten agreement that teachers may manhandle children while children may not make any complaint. In a thoroughgoing adult-centred school – to carry the idea to its logical conclusion – children would have to do preps but staff would not have to mark them, huge classes would work silently under the supervision of one teacher doing a crossword puzzle, and all organisation between lessons would be done by efficient prefects.

Although this last picture is exaggerated, it is not without echoes of reality. However, I don't seriously believe that anyone considers that the primary purpose of education is either to relieve parents of the burden of child-care or to provide schoolteachers with painless employment. Adult-centredness, though it is a sufficiently identifiable ideal to justify a name, is not a serious contender as the purpose of education.

2. SOCIETY-CENTRED EDUCATION

Society-centred education is not merely a serious contender, it is probably the victor. In this system the purpose of education is to produce useful citizens. Rousseau had no time for it, as we have seen. He said, 'You must make your choice between the man and the citizen; you cannot train both.' Let us see how far modern British schools are in fact devoted to training citizens.

O-Level tests were devised to test the top 20% of the school population, and C.S.E. tests were to overlap O-Level and include the next 40%. In the desperate search for qualifications, much larger proportions of children are now entered. About 40% of our children either never take exams, or else take them and fail them. The average result is supposed to be C.S.E. Grade 4, which many employers regard as worthless.

Nevertheless most of us still see the examination system as the ultimate educational objective. If you pass enough exams you are qualified to do things. From the point of view of the individual parent or child the reason for seeking qualification is personal advantage. From the point of view of employers exams are a screening device. From the point of view of society they are a means of persuading as many children as possible to learn about particular areas.

Yet, in spite of the continually rising numbers of children passing exams, society requires more citizens with a high degree of literacy than ever before and schools are therefore blamed for falling standards. When the nation is short of engineers, people say that the schools should be teaching engineering; when industry has a bad image among school-leavers it is the schools that ought to change, not industry. As an ultimate absurdity, when there is severe unemployment, the schools are advised to teach their pupils to become more employable.

This last observation shows how deeply committed we are to the idea that education is education for work. In a time of severe unemployment you would have thought that children would be preparing themselves for something other than an orthodox working life. To prepare for work even harder than before, and then to be refused it when you leave school, is to be thrust into a position of failure and aimlessness; it seems as if the despondency of our young unemployed must be a hidden objective of the system.

School work that is not directed towards examinations is almost always regarded as unimportant. P.E., art and music are sometimes described as 'release' subjects, which presumably means that everything else is a kind of imprisonment. You are released for your own pleasure, but you are imprisoned for the benefit of society.

Outside the classroom children may be expected to learn about leadership and obedience, initiative, self-discipline, team spirit and approved behaviour. A pupil who excelled in all these, as well as demonstrating sufficient intelligence to pass exams, would surely become an ideal citizen. To become an ideal human being this ideal citizen would also need to acquire concern for and understanding of other people, a capacity for joy, a justified self-confidence and a true judgement of moral and aesthetic values, among other things. Schools may try to develop such qualities too, but to the ardent believer in society-centred education they must seem of minor importance.

3. VALUE-CENTRED EDUCATION

Value-centred education is the only alternative to child-centred education that is at all attractive to me. It can be made attractive to anyone – but too much depends on the values you choose.

The principle is that there are certain moral and aesthetic values which have been discovered by civilization and must be handed on from one generation to another. It is possible to accept this principle whether you believe the values should be democratic or aristocratic, whether you favour patriotism or pacifism, whether your aesthetic view is romantic or classical.

Among the teachers in schools since the early nineteenth century there have been plenty of wise moralists and intellectual giants. Presumably they have tried to pass on the highest moral and aesthetic ideas. Unfortunately the lessons learnt by most of their pupils have been utterly philistine; scholars and artists and philanthropists, though they have appeared, have been the exception rather than the rule.

Rudyard Kipling's *Stalky & Co.*, in spite of its sentimental portrayal of a saintly headmaster who really understands boys, gives a brilliant account of the contrast between values ostensibly taught and values actually learned. The masters want the boys to be obedient, respectful, industrious and conformist. The boys admire cunning, insolence and independence; they have an aristocratic horror of a man who shoots a fox, and a similarly aristocratic ease in hobnobbing with the lower classes, in the persons of Foxy the Marshal and Mary and Mother Yeo at the dairy. Apart from Beetle the central trio are at best indifferent to literature. Although they intervene in one serious case of bullying, their method of dealing with bullies is disturbingly sadistic, and they are ruthless in their dealings with fags. Almost the only value the masters and boys share is loyalty, whether to friends, house or nation, but even patriotism has to be rightly handled; when a visiting speaker unfurls a Union Jack at the climax of a speech the boys are embarrassed and hostile.

Throughout the book it is clear that the boys have a sense of values of their own, and that what the staff does has very little influence on it. Their values, of which Kipling seems to approve, appear to me to be on the whole despicable, but that is beside the point. Where I think Kipling was right is in showing that instruction, though it can be an effective way of imparting information, is not an effective way of imparting values.

We are inclined to separate what we want to do from what we have to do. When teachers or exam syllabuses oblige children to read certain books the children will expect to find the reading a disagreeable chore. Even at university I used to find the set books by any author less interesting than his other works. If you feel mildly hostile to most teachers, and a teacher tells you before you see it that a picture is beautiful or a film marvellous, you are likely to find fault with it. If you are told, moreover, that you *ought* to admire some particular work, your tendency to dislike it will probably be even more marked, just as the boys in *Stalky & Co.* could not bear to be told that they *ought* to be patriotic. Values cannot be forced on you by moral pressure. The only way to acquire them is by discovering them for yourself.

4.   GROUP-CENTRED EDUCATION

Group-centred education is a direct response to the idea of child-centred education. The most important thing you can teach, the theory goes, is how to work with others, how to cooperate, how to be a useful member of a group. There is much talk of community spirit.

In the public schools this sort of thing used to happen without anyone thinking much about it. Boys were grouped into houses that competed against each other, so they identified with their houses. Their school also competed with other schools, so they were loyal to a larger group too. Once a day the entire school, staff and pupils, would assemble in chapel, and no boy could fail to notice that he was only one among many.

It seems to be an assumption of those who favour group-centred education that children, if not combined, will scatter in irresponsible individuality. In fact children *want* to be together, *want* to share interests, *enjoy* organising themselves into large-scale games. They may need practice in working together, but they do not need artificial grouping systems to make them want to do so.

It is only too easy for the encouragement of group identification to become highly undesirable, and it is at least arguable that the real responsibility of educationists should be to *oppose* the children's inclination to combine. In support of this view, let me quote Arthur Koestler (from *The Ghost in the Machine*, Hutchinson, 1976):

'The selfish impulses of man constitute a much lesser historic danger than his integrative tendencies. To put it in the simplest way: the individual who indulges in an excess of aggressive self-assertiveness incurs the penalties of society – he outlaws himself, he contracts *out* of the hierarchy. The true believer, on the other hand, becomes more closely knit *into* it; he enters the womb of the church, or party, or whatever the social holon to which he surrenders his identity. For identification in this primitive form always entails a certain impairment of individuality, an abdication of the critical faculties and of personal responsibility.'

It is such group identifications and abdications of personal responsibility that result in religious and ideological wars, concentration camps, torture and genocide. The selfish impulses are harmless by comparison.

'Immersion in the group mind,' says Koestler, 'is a kind of poor man's self-transcendence.' It is a relief to be taken out of oneself. There are certain types of self-transcendence that are of the highest merit. For example, we can become absorbed in a

discussion, or in sympathy with another person, or in listening to music, or in delight in the sunlight. Rather than encouraging group identification, perhaps teachers should be concentrating on such experiences as these.

5.   CHILD-SUPPRESSIVE EDUCATION

Child-suppression is a reaction against child-centredness. According to this view, if you concentrate on the individual child you teach her an exaggerated idea of her own importance; you teach her selfishness and conceit. To concentrate on a child is to spoil her.

Assuming that neglect is not considered a desirable alternative to spoiling, there seem to me to be three approaches consistent with child-suppression. The first is absolute rigidity, the second is rigidity moderated by adult whim, and the third is to put adult needs before children's needs. All three approaches are widely used.

You cannot spoil a child if everything you do or the child does is governed by rigid rules. Where the child transgresses, you must inflict due punishment, no matter how much you feel that it hurts you more than it hurts her. There can be no complaining, and whatever other qualities they acquire the children will certainly not be spoilt. Instead, they are put in a position where cunning in evading rules is advantageous to them, as is lying to keep out of trouble. They will probably regard adults as enemies, and they will almost certainly acquire an irrational respect for rules as opposed to generosity, affection or their own judgement. When they find themselves in a situation where the rules do not apply, they will have no guidelines.

Rigidity modified by adult whim has very different results. If, by keeping the master in a good mood, the boys can persuade him to allow them out five minutes early, they are likely to try to keep him in a good mood. Then, because he lets them out early, they are grateful to him, and appreciate him as an individual apart from the system. When he suddenly

Cooperation is a better basis than authority for a relationship between children of different ages.

75

announces that instead of doing Latin they are all going to go for a walk by the river because it is such a nice day, their admiration is unbounded. His occasional interruptions of routine have a disproportionate influence, and his pupils are made to look on the routine with new eyes. By imitating the teacher, who is no longer an enemy, they may even learn to make judgements of their own.

This is probably more or less how things are with the best and most successful conventional teachers. (I mean 'successful' in terms of the general education of their pupils, rather than specific instruction.) The adult is the centre of everything. This is often a happy situation, but it is a false one. The adult's whims are not the most important aspect of the children's lives; the work itself is more important, one hopes; the children's whims are just as valuable as his; the children's needs are more important than his whims. It is not good for children to depend on somebody else for every initiative, or for them to have to accept somebody else's evaluation of their own ideas. The best atmosphere attainable in a classroom run like this is one of contented sycophancy. There are higher things to aim for.

The third approach to child-suppressive education is to act on the assumption that adults' needs are always more important than children's. This assumption is so obviously false that children automatically reject it, and in doing so are likely to deny that adults' needs are ever more important than their own. They learn only that adults are unreasonable and best avoided.

I think the main reason so many people favour child-suppressive methods, apart from sheer self-centredness or idleness, is that they misunderstand the concept of spoiling. Spoiling is not a consequence of an excess of attention, but of

Many educators used to think it their Christian duty to repress individuality. At least superficially they often succeeded, because children tend to accept any system imposed on them. Modern assemblies may not look as grim as this one, but child-suppression in less obvious form still has its advocates.

wrong attention. It is frequently the result of an adult's desire to get rid of a tiresome child: 'Yes, darling, here's 50 pence. Go and buy yourself something to eat.' This seems more like buying the child off than concentrating on his needs.

It is perfectly consistent with the idea of concentrating on a particular child to refuse to do something the child wants done. In a genuinely affectionate relationship it is absurd for either partner to dominate the other. Cooperation is the objective, and the task in which cooperation is required is the education of each individual child.

6.   ADULTISM

I use the word 'adultism' to mean the assumption that adults are superior to children in every important respect. If this is the case it is obviously foolish for an adult, who knows so much, to be directed by the fancy of a child, who knows so little. It is the duty of the adult to lead the child into the right paths that adults recognise but about which children cannot yet know.

If the adultist assumption is false, perhaps the child's fancy should be allowed to direct the adult, at least in areas where the child knows best. And it is my contention that the adultist assumption *is* false, based on the mistaken notion that knowledge and experience, two areas in which adults plainly excel, are more important than any other qualities.

This notion has extraordinary influence in the adult world outside education, where promotion is largely dependent on age, and the heads of industry, government, church and law are often plainly past their prime. Athletes are forced to retire when their skills begin to decline; practical men of affairs, whose skills are less clearly measurable, are allowed to progress into positions of greater and greater influence. It is not surprising that children in schools, at the bottom of the ladder of age, should be considered generally inferior.

Children are, in fact, superior in many different ways. They are more intuitive, more aware of their immediate surroundings, more responsive to other people, more imaginative and inquisitive, and they have more moral fervour. There are many things which young people know and understand through instinct, intelligence or imagination that older people only remember as pieces of information. In time we may all come to appreciate this; in Ronald Blythe's survey of old people, *The View in Winter* (published by Allen Lane in 1979), a retired schoolmaster says, 'It is strange that we should think our boyhoods immature; they certainly don't appear so when one is very old.'

Whatever general superiorities a child may or may not have, she certainly knows more about her own state of mind than anyone else. Only she herself can say whether she is hungry, or whether she is bored, or whether she has a wonderful idea for a picture, or where it is she needs help. The adult is indeed in general more knowledgeable, and it is precisely for that reason that he can be of use to her. It is the child's role to present the problem and the adult's role to help her find a solution.

Knowledge can be stored in the memory of a computer. It is not a human skill, but a mechanical amassing of data. It is curious that adultists seem to esteem human beings who tend to resemble machines above those who live more vividly. Just as machines should be used by people, and not people directed by machines, so should teachers be used by children, and not children directed by teachers. Just as people deliberately accept instructions from machines (whether they are actually formulated in words, as in some computer programs, or merely implied by the situation, as when a lift stops at your floor, the car demands a gear-change or the alarm-clock tells you to get up), so children should deliberately accept instructions from teachers.

In fact, whatever adultist teachers may feel, there can be no instruction without the child's consent. It may be hard won, or it may be given without question, but unless the child agrees to learn, however reluctantly, no learning can take place.

THERE IS NO ALTERNATIVE

To sum up, people who think education should not be centred around the needs of the individual child misunderstand the needs of the child.

If you think a child needs (and wants) to be aimless, greedy, dishonest, rude, idle and ignorant, then you can be excused for thinking that schools must strive to educate children away from their natural bent.

If on the other hand you agree that children need (and want) to be purposeful, constructive and well-informed, to develop talents and follow up interests and generally to be useful members of the human race, then your role is not to destroy their individuality or to force them to undertake particular activities, but to help them to develop, to explore their own talents and interests and to acquire the skills they need.

Either of these approaches produces confirmation of its own premises.

It is a natural human reaction to resist force. If you try to force children to learn they will be reluctant to do so. By the mere act of seeking to compel virtue, you in fact encourage vice. Anyone who tries to educate by compulsion, then, will find his fears about the childish character confirmed.

A school which starts from the opposite point of view will find that its pupils react well to the interest taken in them, and that, as expected, they take a genuinely positive attitude towards their own education.

There may well be doubts as to which method places heavier demands upon *teachers*, but there seems to be none at all as to which has the preferable results for the *children*.

Are progressive ideals too negative?

Some critics of progressive schools do not object to the concept of child-centredness. What worries them is the fact that progressive ideals seem to be almost entirely negative. Progressive schools are against patriotism and compulsory religion, the feeling goes, but what are they *for*? Freedom of thought seems to such people to be an uncomfortable vacuum, and they want to fill this vacuum in various ways in order to justify the progressive approach to education.

People who are attracted to progressive schools are by definition people who do not accept generally accepted opinions. It is probably not just on education that they hold minority views; they may also be vegetarians, members of C.N.D., health-foodists, extreme leftists, crafts-people, meditators or humanists. Even the crankiest have a right to their opinions. But when, in an effort to counter the contention that progressive ideals are not sufficiently affirmative, they embody their special views in an educational system, that system can no longer be truly progressive. It is unprogressive, I believe, even to impose *negative* ideals on children.

I once knew a young girl whose father was a convinced atheist. She drove him frantic by using her position at a boarding school to go to church every Sunday. Anyone genuinely in favour of free thinking would find this quite acceptable: you do not necessarily discourage religion by refusing to make it compulsory. Similarly, a teacher who was doing myths with a class of 11-year-olds has told me that he was confronted by an enraged mother after he had read them the story of the Creation from Genesis. She had chosen her child's school because there was no religious instruction, she said, and she was not going to allow it. Such parents fail to see that a denial of religion is just as much an act of faith as an assertion of it.

Some years ago the head of one progressive school, who could have been expected to allow freedom of expression to all his staff, nevertheless found himself obliged to get rid of a proselytising communist. It was not that he disagreed with the man's views, he explained, but that he disagreed with the idea of one person's political views being forced on another, particularly a child.

The younger the child, the greater the danger of implanting opinions. The Jesuits felt they could guarantee the permanent Catholicism of any child that came to them before the age of 7. Children are eager to accept the views of anyone they admire, and feel secure when they imitate them. Most general opinions of children, as opposed to those of adolescents, are directly taken from their parents, and many adolescent views are deliberately assumed contradictions of their parents'. For both these reasons it is important to avoid instilling irrational beliefs that the child cannot understand. The child must learn to develop judgement rather than obedience, and the adolescent should have no need to reject responsible attitudes merely because they have been presented as edicts rather than rational behaviour.

Nevertheless, runs the counter-argument, if you do not teach religion, you must teach something else in its place. Throughout the history of progressive education there has been a strong tendency towards neo-pastoralism: the belief that tilling the soil is the closest you can get to ultimate truth and reality. It is part of that belief that you should till the soil with as little mechanical aid as possible, and if you want to thresh corn you should do it with a hand-flail. With the recent fashions for self-sufficiency and alternative energy, the neo-pastoralists have risen again in national esteem, and there is a great alternative ethic that says, 'Thou shalt not eat junk food,' and 'Thou shalt not use chemical fertilizers.'

'ALTERNATIVE' SCHOOLS

The collection of attitudes that goes with this approach has become so clearly defined in some people's minds that they spell the word 'alternative' with a capital A, and want to have

Alternative Schools. Such schools will not merely offer an alternative to conventional education, they will instruct children in particular Alternative Values. Fish-farming, solar heating and natural fertilizers will take important places in the curriculum. There will be instruction in meditation techniques and fringe medicine. Pacifism, mysticism and a general anti-technology will be essential parts of the school's philosophy. Astrology will appear on the time-table, and the word 'community' will acquire a new intensity of meaning. There will be much organised physical contact between people.

Everyone must recognize this Alternative package nowadays. Almost everyone must find something attractive among the many ideas, even if it is only as vague a notion as preferring the country to the town. Similarly, almost everyone must find parts of the package utterly absurd; even within the Alternative movement there are people who jib at Benjamin Creme with his Messiah about to emerge from the Himalayas, and different schools of meditation are as disdainful of one another as different religions. Acupuncture masseurs disapprove of reflexology, which is massage through the feet only; an interest in ley-lines is no guarantee of a belief in reincarnation. Nevertheless the Alternative people have enough in common to recognize each other, and many of them would welcome a full-blooded Alternative School.

The trouble with any such proposal is that it inevitably has overtones of moral compulsion. There is a feeling that a space in the school's philosophy needs to be filled, and an idea is eagerly brought forward to fill it. I do not think that the philosophy of a progressive school has room for *any* dictated creed.

SOCIAL CONSCIENCE AS AN IDEAL

A former headmaster of Dartington Hall, Royston Lambert, was concerned about what he saw as a moral vacuum in the school's philosophy, and he set out to fill it by introducing a number of reforms that most of us at first found intoxicating. Lambert's moral drive was a social one; he wanted the advantages of Dartington education to be available to every-body, and he wanted the supposedly isolated and aloof pupils of Dartington to learn something about life as it is lived by the less affluent. He set about this in three ways: by moving the nursery school into the centre of the village and arranging to share premises and staff with a new state nursery school; by forming links with Northcliffe Comprehensive School in Conisbrough, a mining village in South Yorkshire; and by sending selected pupils to Sicily, where they lived and worked as peasants for six months.

The private nursery school was soon completely absorbed by the state nursery. Some years later we realised that there was still a demand for a different kind of nursery school, and started up again.

The Sicily scheme was short-lived, but while it lasted it had an enormous impact on the children who took part. Most of them had their lives altered by the experience, and when they came back to England few of them found it easy to attach importance once again to things they had come to see as trivial, such as examination work or ordinary social living in a wealthy society. Whether this means that the experience was valuable or damaging depends on your point of view; it was certainly demanding, and the children learnt from the inside about a world most of us know almost nothing about.

The Yorkshire scheme involved short courses with pupils from either school visiting the other, and 12 Northcliffe sixth-formers came to Dartington each year as boarders, paid for partly by their local education authority, partly by the Darting-ton Hall Trust and partly by their own parents. Financial problems have brought the sixth-form courses to an end, but the short-term courses still continue; Dartington people regard them as a sort of social-studies programme, and Northcliffe people look upon Dartington as a useful base for environ-mental work as well as an opportunity to give children the experience of living away from home.

So ended Royston Lambert's attempts to build a social conscience into the central philosophy of the school. It is unusual for an expensive private school to go to such lengths to submit its pupils to ordinary state education or Italian peasant life, but it is not an essentially 'progressive' idea. There are plenty of good ideas in education that can be put into practice equally well in conventional or progressive schools, and Lambert's ideas were of that kind. They did not fill an apparent 'moral vacuum'.

CREEDS MEAN CONFORMITY

There are many schools that are based on creeds that take the place of the public school's patriotism and obedience. The Krishnamurti School at Brockwood Park near Petersfield, for instance, is run on monastic lines, and every pupil has to undertake to abide by certain rules before being admitted. Steiner schools, which exist all over Europe, are governed by a weird series of prescriptions about everything from art materials – at a certain age, for instance, Steiner children may only use poster paints in primary colours, and only on *wet paper* – to dance styles, curriculum and leisure activities. Steiner-school children may not learn to read until nearly 7, and watching television and listening to recorded music are firmly discouraged.

St. Christopher Letchworth is vegetarian, and has a morning assembly that is not associated with any particular religion but seems to have a religious intention. Quaker schools are said to have much in common with the progressive movement, and certainly the religion has a comparable absence of dogma. Nevertheless, the Quaker schools seem to require a conformity from their pupils that their beliefs do not demand from adults.

If the essential progressive school does not demand any such attitudes from its children, what *are* its distinguishing values? I shall provide extensive answers to that question in the chapters that follow. But I am convinced that the basic structure of true progressive education rests firmly on the refusal to impose a particular set of values on the school's pupils. This is as strong a philosophical position as to insist on imposing one. The rejection of imposition is what fills the gap that so many people try to fill with their own particular beliefs. That is why any attempts to fill the gap in any other way are bound to fail as long as a school remains true to its progressive ideal.

To refuse to impose particular values is not the same as to deny them. Children express opinions all the time. Young children, indeed, are inclined to judge largely according to their parents' prejudices. They need to be presented with different points of view, and they need to be allowed to choose. To impose a single point of view, no matter how virtuous, may teach obedience or it may teach rebellion; to *offer* a point of view develops the child's personal judgement.

In a video documentary of Dartington Hall there is a sequence

showing an argument between a student who is preparing her C.S.E. art work and an art teacher. They disagree about the value of what she is planning, and towards the end of the discussion the teacher says, 'I'm not going to stop you doing it, but I'm not exactly going to give you any encouragement.' After the vigour of the argument, this is not a weak surrender, but a clear statement of the real position: He has advised the girl not to do what she proposes, but the final decision is hers to make.

On the broader fields of social values and philosophy, too, the final decision must always remain with the children.

ACCENTUATING THE POSITIVE

What then are the positive ideals of progressive education? I have already said that respect for the child is at the heart of any successful progressive approach. Where mutual respect exists, four other goals are within our reach: (1) We can help children take *pleasure* in learning; (2) we can give them *time* to develop at their own pace; (3) we can help them towards a healthy moral and psychological outlook; and (4) we can accompany them in the vital search for *truth*.

In the following chapters I shall discuss those goals and how they are best achieved.

A friendly relationship between pupils and teachers is a universal ideal of progressive educators. Persuasion takes the place of authority.

Learning as pleasure: Countesthorpe

The ground is cleared for a full discussion of the good things that progressive education can do for today's children. This chapter is a factual account, rather than a theoretical exposition, of a school whose pupils really *enjoy* the learning process. Moreover, in these pages I shall show progressive methods at work – and strikingly successful – not in an expensive boarding school but in an unselective state school.

Most school administrators seem to believe that learning is a painful drudge, or else they have organised their schools in an extraordinarily unsuitable way. Going to school is compulsory, and a set curriculum is usually compulsory and children are punished for not doing preps. The attempt is made to motivate children by competition, by promotion prospects and by the chance of winning gold stars or prizes, but seldom by persuading them that the work they are doing is useful or interesting. Often additional work is set as a punishment, and what is set as a punishment at one moment can hardly be presented as a pleasure the next. It seems clear that to most people concerned with education learning is a sour, weary business and children have to be driven or cajoled through it by threats, sanctions and bribery.

There are teachers, though, who have more sensible views. At Countesthorpe College, near Leicester, they broke up the traditional structure of classes and insisted on every child following an individual, self-chosen course of study. I have visited the school twice, both times in ways designed to give me a deeper sense of the school than the usual chat and walk round; first I joined the school for one day as a teacher, then for three days as a pupil. I was immensely impressed.

Countesthorpe is not a private school; it is a local comprehensive. In spite of the anxieties of parents and the supervision
of the local education authority, it has managed for some years
to take the ideals of progressive education an enormously
important stage further than any independent institution I
know of. I shall describe it as I saw it.

My first visit was during the early days when students were
still allowed to play radios during lesson time and there was a
fair amount of vandalism, including, in the part of the school I
visited, a frequent blocking of the lavatories. For my day's
teaching I had a small group of 14- or 15-year-olds who wanted
to start a rock group. We were given a music room for the day,
and produced one rock and roll song which was reasonably
performable by four o'clock. The delightful part of the day for
me was not the work we did, but the instantly easy relationship
with the children. They knew more about the school than I did,
so they, to some extent, felt they had to look after me; I knew
more about music and song-writing than they did, so they
wanted to listen to what I had to say. Socially we were on an
equal footing, and they were able to speak to me as a normal
person. This is extremely unusual in schools, where almost all
visitors are treated as a foreign but definitely superior race.

This admirable equality is not the subject of this chapter, but
it is a prerequisite for the style of learning that went on in the
school. There were plenty of other remarkable things about
Countesthorpe – the democratic system of government, the
dealing with the problem of vandalism by instantly clearing up
the consequences, the tremendous dedication of the teachers –
but it is on the style of learning that I want to concentrate.

At schools like St. Christopher and Dartington most lessons
are still taken by a teacher standing in front of a class, literally
and metaphorically. It is mainly the social atmosphere that
warrants the label 'progressive'. Countesthorpe has the same
social atmosphere, but it has extended the progressive ideal into
the learning situation as well.

Children come to Countesthorpe at 14. Instead of being
divided into forms they are put into what they call 'pods', each
with a hundred or so children and four or five teachers. The
intake is comprehensive and there is no streaming. The pod I
joined as a teacher on my first visit was a large, irregularly
shaped room, divided by shelves and working tables, and

carpeted; it had two classrooms attached to it, one for art and one for science. As well as being in a particular pod each child had a particular tutor, and it was this tutor who helped to sort out the individual timetables, and who was responsible for the child's English, social studies and maths. When their timetables were complete the children went out of the pod for several lessons each day, but when they had nothing else timetabled they came back for what was called Team Time. (Although each child had a particular tutor, the teachers in the pod worked as a team, and one might take extra responsibility for maths, say, or art.) In Team Time the children worked individually at their own pace, and hardly any two children were working on the same project.

My three days as a pupil were in the middle of the autumn term some three years later, and were spent in a pod with 15-year-olds who were to be taking their exams in the summer. I should stress that what I saw was not necessarily *the* Countesthorpe approach, but only the approach of one particular team.

THE TWO STRUCTURES

In a recent book, *The Enquiring Classroom* (Falmer Press, 1984), Stephen Rowland makes an interesting distinction between two types of learning activity, which he calls Structures A and B. In Structure A the activity proceeds in the following way:

(1) Children select stimuli to which they respond.
(2) Children set task.
(3) They develop particular concepts/skills required by the task.

Here is how the activity progresses in Structure B:

(1) Teacher decides skills/concepts.
(2) Teacher designs/sets appropriate task.
(3) Child performs task.
(4) Child acquires specified learning.

In A, says Rowland, 'the links between the stages take place naturally and there is no question of the appropriateness of the skills/concepts to their activity. Nor is there any question of interpretation of the task or its interest value. Once the sequence has begun it is limited only by the extent of the children's present experience and knowledge, but it serves to extend both.'

The principal drawback of B is that the child might not interpret and internalise the nature of the task as the teacher intended, for a variety of reasons – for instance, present experience, lack of interest or poor design of task.

The principal problem of A is thought to be a need to ensure that the children develop a comprehensive range of skills and knowledge. In fact, though, all that is necessary is that they should develop an adequate range, and probably no two people actually need the same assortment. I had long talks with several 15-year-olds about social-studies projects they were doing at Countesthorpe, and those interviews gave me a good idea of the sort of skills and knowledge they were acquiring as they pursued their learning according to Structure A.

There are three points that I hope will become clear from these interviews. First, every timetable was individually planned (I just give two examples in the following summaries of four interviews). If you consider that all these children were in one group, the range of possibilities is astonishing. Secondly, the children had been helped to choose projects that meant something to them personally; they were involved in their work in a way that is virtually impossible in a conventional class-room. Thirdly, the range of acceptable subjects for a social-studies project is infinite.

GARY AND HIS PROJECTS

Gary's Timetable

Monday	Art	French	Science	Team	Team	Team
Tuesday	Team	Team	Eng.Lit	French	Maths	German
Wednesday	Team	Biology	Science	Team	German	French
Thursday	Art	Art	German	Eng.Lit	Maths	Team
Friday	Team	German	Team	Drama	Drama	Drama

Gary's main project for social studies was a study of children's imagination. It was to be in three sections, the first about children from 2 to 5 in a crèche, then from 5 to 7 in an infant school, and finally in a junior school. He started by wanting to go to a near-by crèche to help out, and his project had been just to keep a diary. He became interested and wanted to find out how children decided what to do. In the crèche he watched the games they played and the repetition they

enjoyed. At an infant school he saw how they developed ideas, reading, playing games, making up stories, drawing and making models. He was working with some juniors now.

He was also doing these other pieces of course work:

1. A child study on a 3-year-old who lived next door. It started because of the interest Gary took in the crèche. So far he had three sections in mind – one about the little boy's reaction to an imaginary robot in his wardrobe which Gary had invented and found hard to disinvent; one involving a general comparison between his subject and the standards given in a published child-development chart ('He talks really well. He is ahead in some things and not in others'); and one about the TV programmes and books that the 3-year-old liked. Gary expected more ideas to develop.

2. The library. Gary went twice a week to the library to get books out, usually fiction, and had decided to learn more about the place. He arranged with a library assistant to work there for a morning, and he had found out about how they order books, how to use the microfiche machine and how to book out, and about the way books in a library are arranged.

3. His play. He had written a play for young children called 'The Golden Apples of Glob', and he and some friends had rehearsed it and performed it at a number of local schools. He had enjoyed seeing kids enjoy his play, and it made him feel he had achieved something. He had learnt that you had to plan a play before you wrote it, otherwise it dragged on and on. His original plan had changed in the course of writing. It would have been a bit boring without the songs, which the audience really enjoyed. And he had now started to write a new play.

Gary said work was all right when you got into it, but hard to get down to. He did most of his work at home. He liked writing plays and poems, and his favourite subject was drama.

His interest in young children was sincere, thoughtful and

Children are generally better motivated when trying to find answers to their own questions than when merely being fed information. Progressive schools tend to believe that this is the best way to acquire social values as well as knowledge.

mature. What he was studying was of real importance to him, and he was learning at first hand, forming his own conclusions, using published material only when it was necessary to help him analyse his own experience. This is usually thought of as the working style of an adult – and an adult of superior intelligence, at that.

His library work was in a sense more conventional in that he had gone to the library and been taught about it, but he had gone there because he was interested, not because a teacher told him to go, and he had gone on his own and had learnt by experience. Once again this seems an adult way of acquiring information: You acquire knowledge because you want it, not because someone says you need it.

The play, finally, was an ideal exercise for someone who wished eventually to become an actor. Already at 15 he had had the experience of writing, directing and acting in a play, which had been performed publicly on several occasions. This was not something that had been squeezed in after school, it was an important part of his school day; the school recognized the personal importance of the play to him and his actors. The usual conflict between the individual's needs and school's requirements simply did not exist.

There was never any homework demanded at Countesthorpe, and yet Gary said he did most of his work at home. There could hardly be a clearer indication of commitment.

LESLEY'S PROJECTS

Lesley's Timetable

Monday	Art	Art	Art	Team	Maths	Team
Tuesday	Team	Team	Music	Dress-making	Dress-making	Dress-making
Wednesday	Science	Team	Team	Science	Science	Team
Thursday	Team	Team	Dress-making	Team	Team	Team
Friday	Team	Maths	Team	Art	Art	Art

These were Lesley's course-work projects:
1. People who really impressed her. This was her Mum's idea. She was writing about Marilyn Monroe, Zandra Rhodes and David Bowie. She was not just putting down what she knew about them, but mainly her feelings and reactions. She wrote poems about them.

2. Addiction. People had visited the school and given talks, and her tutor was running a group on the subject. She was getting information from the library and writing off for pamphlets.

3. Blacks in a white society. After working on drugs she became interested in people who don't fit in. She was writing about people being persecuted, mostly using her own ideas, but she was interested in other people's feelings about race. Her Grandad and other old people she knew were very prejudiced against blacks, but younger people didn't seem to mind.

4. School life. She had written about her life at Countesthorpe because she was having such a good time, meeting all the lads and feeling important. She wrote poems and stories and accounts of things she and her friends had done, like practising in the music block or mucking about. I asked her what she had learnt from doing this and she said she had learnt to try and get some work done instead of skiving off early; because she had written down what she did, and because of what she felt when she read it, she thought she should behave differently.

5. A comparison between her Mum's life and the life of a model. She had thought of writing about it herself because her Mum was always going on about it, and she had found an article on a model's life in the *Sunday Times* Magazine.

Lesley had not liked her previous school because it was so strict. The girls had not been allowed nail-polish or earrings. There was no swearing and everyone had to be dead quiet. They were given lines and detentions as punishment. It was different at Countesthorpe because if you know you can get away with something you don't bother in the first place.

When she finished the year Lesley hoped to work as a masseuse or something to do with beauty. If she didn't get a job she would stay at school.

What is striking about Lesley's choice of topics is that most of them are strongly personal. Probably no one else would choose to write about Zandra Rhodes, Marilyn Monroe and David Bowie. Certainly no one else could describe Lesley's life at school, or compare her Mum's life to that of a model. These are not subjects that would normally be taught at school, yet for Lesley they were important, and in studying them she was learning to understand the world. Her own comments on her school-life project make this clear; her words actually influenced her behaviour. One project was about her mother, and another was suggested by her mother. Her grandfather featured in her project on black people. The world she lived in at home was the same as the world she studied at school – a situation which is all too rare in conventional education.

Like all the other children I interviewed, Lesley was a prolific writer. O-Level is intended only for the top 20% of the population, but at Countesthorpe over 50% of the children regularly achieve O-Level grades in English Language and Social Studies. Encouraging children to follow up their own interests helps them to understand the value of study; it also shows them the importance and satisfaction of the ability to express yourself in words.

These children were developing their understanding of the world, learning things that meant something to them and acquiring opinions based on observation and not hearsay. In doing these vital things instead of studying set topics they were not losing out in terms of general skills; they were actually doing far better than children in conventional schools.

ANGELA'S FAMILY TREE

Angela's main project was the working out of her family tree. She had managed to work back to 1584, and had tracked down one ancestor before that – a matter of 14 or 15 generations. She had learnt a lot about the records office and archives, and the differences between then and now – for instance, in the size of families.

She had enjoyed doing it, because she had only done writing projects before and had wanted to do something different. This had involved going out of school and seeing real archives. She had also been round visiting cousins she had never met before, sometimes accompanied by her Mum. She had been working on the project for a year and a few months now. Her Grandad told her a lot. Sometimes she had found her ancestors' jobs in the archives. Most of them had been labourers, but they always lived in the same village.

The family tree itself she had set out on a special large piece of paper. The remembered family history, written on ordinary sheets, went back as far as her Grandad's grandparents. Her Grandad remembered things from different times, so each thing was put on a separate sheet. Most of his memories were of family affairs, not major events like wars. There were accounts of carrying the cake at weddings, wash-days, lighting the copper and so on.

In addition to this Angela was writing about the present-day family and including her Mum's and Dad's biographies. She was interested in the physical resemblance of her cousins, and their jobs and whereabouts. In fact they all still lived near-by.

The idea for this work had come to her when she was doing a project on families and marriage which she dropped because she had lost interest in it. Now she thought she would probably also improve on the original piece of work and include it in her main project.

The project would end with the modern day, but she would also write down how she had gone to the records office and found her information. She would include photographs of present-day people because they showed interesting things about heredity, for instance that all one branch of the family have ginger hair.

Because of my interest in this piece of work we were nearing the end of the period, and I was surprised to find that Angela did not know what time the bell was supposed to go. She only had time to show me one more piece of course work, which was on heart transplants and consisted of a mass of newpaper cuttings and photographs with her own extremely interesting summaries and comments. Then the bell did go.

The family-tree project would never have succeeded in the same way if it had been set as a classroom task. For one thing there could not have been sufficient time. For another, making any task compulsory is to create resistance to it; one of the delights of Angela's interviews with her family was that she had decided to do them herself.

This was personal history, researched at first hand. Angela was the world expert on her subject, and her subject was one that any social historian might have been keen to cover. She had learnt how to draw a family tree and how to use the records office and the archives. She had discovered at first hand some of the changes that take place over the course of history. She had seen how close we are, in terms of generations, to our Tudor ancestors. She had happened on some of the consequences of heredity. She had explored personal memories of her family – something of great importance that no teacher can hope to provide. And above all she had opened up a vast range of possible and interesting inquiry. There was no reason for this project ever to come to an end. It was material for a lifetime.

JAMES AND HIS MAPS

James was working on street names in the centre of Leicester. He had got the idea from a book of suggestions for projects.

First he had got a map of medieval Leicester and a map of modern Leicester, taken an area within a particular boundary and made a list of 36 streets, comparing medieval and modern names. He was finding the reasons for the new names, using the dictionary, his imagination (for such streets as Elbow Lane) and a book from the reference library about famous people in Leicester, which should explain many of the proper names. At present he was reading a chapter on street names in a book called *English Place Names*.

The write-up of the project would include an introduction saying what he had done and giving a general background for the main street names in England. Then would come photo-copied maps and the list of street names in Leicester. After that he would put his reasons for the names, and finally his conclusions – what he had found out and what were the hard parts.

His tutor had found the maps for him, but otherwise it was all his own idea. He felt he had learnt much general information, including a variety of meanings of words (as in Count Street, where 'Count' might refer to a nobleman or a tally) and history as reflected in changes on maps.

His other course work included a study of maps of Leicester through the ages, and of life in 1902. The latter had been his first project, chosen because it was historical but not too ancient (because he wanted to use original sources). It was still not finished. He had just found an autobiography of someone about that time. Before finding this he had been looking through newspapers and writing out the main stories, including local ones from the Leicester *Mercury*. Newpapers give more detail than history books do. In 1902, he had discovered, they had no front page with headlines.

In addition he was working up a major project on conservation, getting his information from books, by writing off to people, from personal knowledge, magazines and stories. He would include his own photographs and would organise the write-up into different sections when his research was finished.

James was a more bookish child than the others I interviewed, and his work, though personally researched, was mostly based on written sources rather than first-hand experience. If you allow children to study whatever interests them, they will not necessarily opt for personal interviews and practical investigation. Some will be fascinated by words and some by books. This is hardly surprising, but there are many teachers who seem to think that no child will handle a book unless forced to.

Yet even bookish James, who obviously enjoyed studying his street maps, was deliberately taking his history from contemporary newpapers rather than school books, and his project on conservation was going to involve photographs of areas that were of particular concern to him. The topics he chose to study were realities to him. He was not amassing a headful of abstract information; he was investigating meaning and importance.

TEACHERS' COMMENTS

At a teachers' team meeting I attended, the teachers were discussing various pieces of social-studies work in order to decide whether to enter the children for O-Level or C.S.E., the difference being that O-Level requires one main project and eight bits of course-work, but C.S.E. requires only one main project. They were also commenting on work by children in various tutor-groups to see what alterations, improvements or additions they might recommend.

They wondered, for instance, whether someone who had written a beautiful piece about visits to an old people's home should be advised to add photographs, and decided it was not necessary. One boy had been going out to an area where there was a lake and a disused canal. He had taken some superb photographs and mounted them in professional-style thick-card frames, and was now writing descriptions. His tutor read one out; it was extremely clear and good. The other members of the team said the photographs would have been good enough for a piece of course-work by themselves, but as the written work was good too they were pleased with the whole project.

They were concerned about whether the variety of course-work undertaken by certain children was adequate, regardless of its merit.

Among the projects mentioned were a minute-by-minute account of a Duke of Edinburgh award walk, with pictures and a map; a diary of a blue-tit, with superb photographs of a blue-tit's nest in the author's garden; and a map showing birds' nests in a certain area, with descriptions of the birds out of books, but descriptions of their habitats from observation. One of the less successful pieces of work was a rather perfunctory account of a child's home area, which was apparently a deadly spot, with a plan of the rectangular park showing swings and slides, plus a questionnaire passed round a few friends to ask how they would improve the park. Someone was working possibly too exclusively on game and shooting, and the boy who had done the two bird projects already mentioned had also done one on fish, which some teachers felt might have been too much the same. The team decided that this was all right, however. One teacher mentioned a girl who had done four pieces of work about her own village – an acceptable specialisation because one was philological, one geographical, one historical and one sociological

The meeting was mainly concerned with examination work, but in spite of that the criteria of judgment seemed valuable; the requirements of the examiners seemed to have been brought astonishingly close to the needs of the children. Nevertheless I should stress my conviction that the value of this kind of work lies mainly in the benefit it brings to the children in itself, not in the examination grade.

I spoke to many Countesthorpe children besides those I have named, and I found the range of intellectual ability comprehensive. They were all proud of their work and ready to talk about it with an extraordinarily articulate and detached self-confidence. The standard of written English was also extremely high. The skills and knowledge the children had acquired were impressive, but more impressive still was their attitude. No one was reluctant to come to school. They knew what they were doing was important, because they were finding answers to their own questions. For all of them learning was a pleasure.

Giving children time

'They are always looking for the man in the child, without thinking what he is before he becomes a man.' I have quoted this sentence from Rousseau in an earlier chapter, and also this one: 'Childhood has its own ways of seeing, thinking and feeling.' We still need to be reminded of these truths.

In spite of the fact that we no longer expect children to behave like small adults, to read only the Bible and *Robinson Crusoe* and to sit patiently for hours enduring incomprehensible grown-up conversation, we still tend to praise them for being, as we see it, more like adults and to condemn them for being true to their age. 'Mature' and 'grown-up' are words of high commendation, and 'infantile' and 'childish' terms of disapproval.

The implication is clear. Although our society tolerates children reading children's books and playing childish games, we would feel much happier if in their general social behaviour they were just like grown-ups. (If we were strictly honest we would have to admit that this is not exactly what we mean, because grown-ups are certainly not consistently considerate, calm, responsible and wise, nor are children always selfish, careless, unrealistic, wild or petulant.)

A great deal of conventional education consists of an effort to shift children out of their childishness as soon as possible. A good many school rules exist only to force children into an 'adult' pattern of behaviour that does not come naturally to them. The hope seems to be that adult behaviour will become a habit, and to that extent part of the child's character.

When the B.B.C. made a film about a progressive school called 'What a Way to Run a School', one of the questions put

Clothes and tradition can force children to mimic adult behaviour instead of naturally living out their childhood.

to the school's headmaster was about freedom. Was it not true that some children took advantage of the freedom they were given and made bad use of it? Yes, he said, it was. He was surprised that anyone could expect children to know all about freedom the moment they were given it. A child who arrived in the school did not know all about O-Level geography, but came to the school to learn. Why should children be expected to know all about freedom?

Children need time to learn. It is a mistake to try to rush them. You learn more from experience than from precept. Often children need the opportunity to learn from their own mistakes.

Even wholeheartedly progressive teachers are inclined to expect children to behave in ways that would be appropriate only if they were older. This is partly because the teachers see the school growing older and yet remaining at about the same stage of behaviour. Any teacher recognises the feeling at the beginning of the autumn term that there are no footballers left, or no musicians, or no real scholars; and every September teachers in every school in the country comment on the comparative immaturity of their pupils. There is even the feeling that a lesson learnt in school one year should automatically still be known the next, and people grumble that certain types of behaviour don't get better from one year to the next. 'But we went over all that last year,' they say, momentarily forgetting that they went over it with a different group of children. They often believe, even if only subconsciously, that it is mainly through the benefit of their instruction that the children are maturing. They forget that children grow up whatever their teachers do. When this year's class seems less mature than last year's, the teacher has an uncomfortable sense of guilt.

For similar reasons lessons are frequently pitched at too high a level for the children being taught. Teachers are too often afraid that they are not getting the children on fast enough, that if they haven't learnt long division by the time they're 10 they will never learn it, that if they aren't stretched they are going to become lazy. In a book entitled *Reading* (Cambridge University Press, 1978), Frank Smith, a specialist in the subject, explains why these worries are mistaken:

'Children will not stay in any situation in which there is nothing for them to learn. Everyone is equipped with a very efficient device that prevents wasting time in situations where there is nothing to learn. That device is called "boredom", and boredom is something all children want to escape. A child who is bored in class is not demonstrating ill will or inability or even sheer cussedness; boredom should convey just one very clear message for the teacher, that there is nothing in the particular situation for the child to learn.

'Unfortunately there are two reasons why there might be nothing for a child to learn in a particular situation, and hence two causes of boredom, which may arise from quite different sources. One reason why children might have nothing to learn is very simple – they know it already. Children will not attend to anything they know already – they will be bored. But children exhibit the same symptoms of boredom not because they know something already, but because they cannot make sense of what they are expected to learn. Children cannot be made to attend to nonsense. It is a teacher's responsibility, not the pupil's, to make sure that what children are expected to learn has the possibility of making sense, not only in terms of what the children know already, but in terms of what they might want to know. Adults might see quite clearly that a certain exercise will improve a child's useful knowledge or skills, but unless the child can see some sense in the exercise, the instruction is a waste of time.'

TOO MUCH TOO SOON

Teachers who want to get children on fast often spend a lot of time on long division with pupils who are too young for it. It is possible to teach able 9-year-olds to set the sums out correctly, to do rough calculations at the right-hand side of the page, to put the answers in the right place and bring down the right numbers, but hardly any of them will understand the meaning behind the performance. Most of them will have to be taught again when they are 10, and again when they are 11, and again just before O-Level, by which time the brightest among them will at last have understood what it is all about. Those of moderate ability will have become so used to writing down numbers with no particular significance that they will never bother to understand the process properly. It would have been better to wait until they were all ready.

Foreign languages are a similar case. The fluency of children brought up in bilingual cultures is often cited to prove that children who start a language very early can acquire a good accent and learn to speak perfectly. In fact the evidence has nothing to do with classroom teaching. In the classroom there is not the same motivation that there is in the home; the child gets the teacher's attention for only a tiny fraction of lesson time, and in any case total lesson time in a full year will probably not be more than a hundred hours. All that the evidence shows is that you learn a language more efficiently by living with people who speak it than you do by studying it in a classroom, whatever your age.

Another frequent requirement is for children to learn about topics that will be useful to them as adults, but are of no interest to them at present – local government, for instance, or home economics. A friend of mine once commented that teachers were bent on teaching what was of importance to them, at whatever age they were, rather than what was important to the pupils. We might as well, he suggested, instruct children in the problems of the menopause and the creative use of retirement.

However, the main reason for the anxious drive to get children on as fast as possible, to fill their minds as full as possible with information, to make them learn accepted opinions by heart, is certainly the examination system.

Examinations are deliberately made so difficult that most children in the relevant age group are not able to do well in them. Yet in a few years, if they were interested, this level of subjects like English or history would come much more easily. I know of a girl who took O-Level geography one year and failed; she did not study geography in the sixth form, but the next year she was entered again by mistake; as she had been entered she thought she might as well sit the exam, and she passed it. No extra study but one year of experience made the difference.

Examinations are set to test the limits of what children can do in certain fields if pushed hard. Obviously some children can and do pass them, at some sort of standard, at the appropriate ages. Even for the most able, the exams involve a great deal of hard work. For the less able, they involve hard work for no reward. Up to five years of the children's lives are largely directed towards a few hours in the examination room. There they are tested either in sheer feats of memory, or else in tasks that they could perform much more easily in a year or two. No wonder teachers think it necessary to drive, drill and dictate.

A.S. Neill paid no attention to exams. If Summerhill children wanted to take O- or A-Levels, they could go to a technical college and take them, and because of their attitude and motivation they would, he believed, have no difficulties. Many of his pupils proved him right. Countesthorpe, by using C.S.E. mode 3 examinations that the teaching staff devised themselves, managed for a time to examine children, in some subjects at least, only in what was useful for them to learn. The examination boards have now begun to interfere.

By contrast with Countesthorpe and Summerhill, most progressive schools accept the domination of the exam system and run conventional timetables. In junior classes the organisation of the day may be fairly informal, but reading, writing and arithmetic are learnt as a matter of course since they are necessary skills that the children enjoy and see to be valuable. From the age of 11 onwards, though, the day is likely to be just as sharply divided as in the most reactionary of public schools: maths, French, break, double art, English, lunch, music, double science, end of school, prep in the evening, more of the same tomorrow.

As long as the examination system persists in its present pattern, teachers will be obliged to drive children on to demonstrate the best they can do in certain limited fields. The exams test what children *can* be made to do in these conditions, but no one asks whether it is what they *ought* to be doing. Not even the children, for the most part, ask whether it is what they ought to be doing. Exams are the passport to higher education or to jobs, and therefore they are not to be questioned.

ACTING YOUR AGE SOCIALLY

Giving children time to learn in the classroom is important; giving children time to learn in their social lives is even more so. After all, to teach a child to quote the editor's description of the characters in a Shakespeare play does no worse than instil

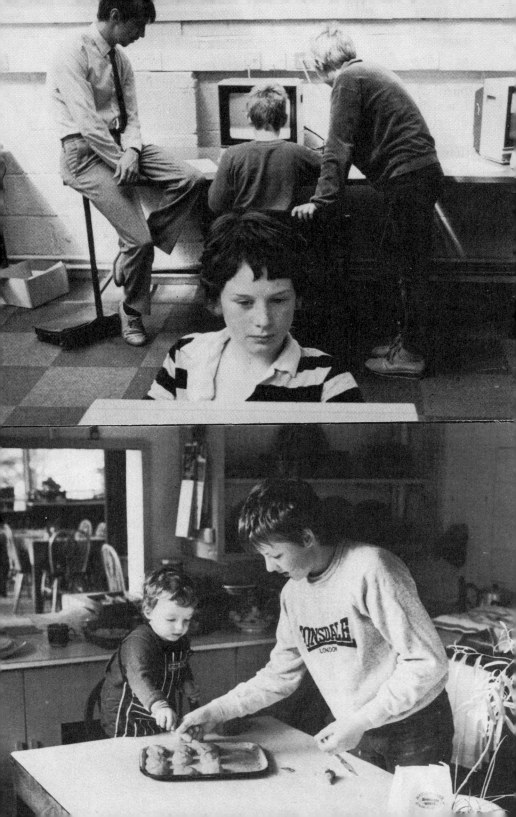

Concentration, essential for rapid learning, comes easily only when you are interested. Music, computer-programming and cake-making all have an immediate appeal; the really skilful teacher can even arouse an individual child's enthusiasm for less alluring studies such as mathematics.

a hatred of Shakespeare; the consequences of demanding adult behaviour from adolescents can be far more damaging.

A child's purpose in life, says the traditional adult view, is to grow up. Sadly enough, this view is accepted by most children. At some ages this is more evident than others, but it takes a strong character to prefer to stay with a younger group when most of the class are going to join an older one. The best age, in a child's eyes, is not adulthood, but just a year or two in advance of one's own.

Unlike adults, who see the advance towards maturity only as a growth in responsibility, children also see growing up as a growth in independence, which can be used responsibly or irresponsibly. Smoking is still a symbol of maturity in the minds of some children, something that grown-ups do but try to dissuade children from doing – and so, obviously, a powerful pleasure for the initiated. To smoke is to say clearly to parents and teachers, 'You can't tell me what I am to do with my life.'

With some young people there is also a sense of pressure to join a more sophisticated and exciting set. 'It's awful, I'm 18 and still a virgin,' I have heard such a young person say. With younger children there is cachet in staying up late and seeing X-films, and some boys of all ages like to show off their knowledge of obscure kinds of alcoholic drink.

These are all examples of the urge to grow up being a damaging one, one that reminds us that 'sophisticated' actually used to mean corrupted or adulterated. Children often want to do what older people do, without realising that they also need to understand what older people understand.

This is rather curious, because children are in fact happier with friends of roughly their age, doing the things appropriate to their age group. Unfortunately, it takes a great deal of confidence to do what you want to do, rather than what your friends (though they may secretly want to do the same as you) think it is tougher or more sophisticated to do.

This slightly showing-off and irresponsible independence is sometimes accompanied by conformity to stuffy adult standards for public behaviour. The star prefect denies his own values and assumes those of the school, which places decorum unrealistically high. There is a type of courtesy to visitors that is impossible to fault, except that it is purely a performance. The message is not 'I am pleased to see you,' or 'How do you do. This is me. I hope we will get on all right together,' or even 'Come on. This is the quickest and most comfortable way of getting where you want to go,' but only 'I know the proper way to behave and this is it.'

In David Benedictus's novel about Eton, *The Fourth of June*, a rebel against the school is tamed by giving him responsibility – in other words, enrolling him to help perpetuate the system. Adults know that when a child is offered the chance of higher status, of rising one more step on the ladder to maturity, he finds the offer very difficult to turn down, even if it is in total opposition to his character and his wishes. Prefects are children thrust into a position of hypocrisy, where they have to punish people for doing things they do or would like to do themselves; and yet in spite of that, children are eager for the position.

HOW TO STOP THE RUSH TO ADULTHOOD

What is to be done about the attractions of unnatural sophistication that appeal to so many children? The difficulty of answering that question is perhaps best illustrated by an anecdote. A few years ago at Dartington Hall Middle School there was a craze for bicycle jumping, and in the road outside the gym some boys had set up a ramp about nine inches high. All through break a 6-year-old boy, cycling round on his little bike with stabilisers, watched them as they sped down the road and leapt into the air. When break was over and they had gone, it was his turn. He pedalled as hard as he could and just managed to get to the top of the ramp; his front wheel dropped over the edge and he was thrown off onto the concrete.

It was my son, and I saw this through a window. Fortunately he was not much hurt, but of course if I had guessed what he wanted to do and had time to stop him I wouldn't have allowed it to happen. The incident illustrates, rather drastically, the disadvantage of learning by one's own mistakes. It is not a pleasant process. There are plenty of things which older people do that young children cannot do. It is not one of the tenets of progressive education that every child should be permitted to do anything at any time!

Ideally, my son should have been warned about the consequences of attempting such a jump, and as long as he believed the warning he would not have wanted to try it. In the same way, at a different level, teenagers need to be warned about the consequences of taking drugs or drinking too much alcohol. Mutual honesty and trust are essential; only if the warnings are over-stated or the approach is bluntly authoritarian will many young people ignore them. Where there is danger, a school has to try to make it unnecessary for children to learn from their own mistakes; the cost is too high.

Another way of giving children *time* to grow up is to provide plenty of opportunity for the sort of play they need. I knew a clever and articulate 11-year-old with elderly parents and grown-up brothers who used to spend most of his free time playing in the sand-pit with children of 6 and 7. At Christmas one of the house-mothers gave him a present. It was that toy with a disc of sandpaper that you can make spin round and strike against flints behind pieces of coloured plastic, so that you get a display of red and blue and green sparks. He was pathetically delighted because he had never had anything like it before. He had missed all the play he should have had when he was younger, and the school fulfilled a need for him.

That same house-mother also kept a dolls' house, and girls of 12 and 13 used to play with it for hours. Boys were more inhibited about it because it takes courage for a boy to stop being tough. Given the chance, many 12-year-olds are more genuinely interested in dolls' houses than in pop music.

You can also discourage fake sophistication by continuing to approve of and show enthusiasm for the kind of behaviour appropriate to the age of the children. If you asked my class of 10-year-olds what they would like you to read to them, some would call for horror stories, or James Bond, or crime novels. But if you gave them what they wanted, most of them along with the other children would be bored. Children of 10 prefer folk tales and children's books, which they listen to with delight.

(When, on the other hand, O-Level English literature comes along and most candidates would be happy to read horror stories, or James Bond, or crime novels, they are required to read Dickens and Shakespeare, and most of the time most of them are bored. *Twelfth Night* and *Oliver Twist* remained unreadable for me for 10 years after my exams. I might never have returned to Dickens if it had not been for one master who advised his class not to read any until we were at least 20. This heretical advice eventually led me back into an appreciation of English literature.)

THE VALUE OF PLAY

Adults ought to approve of play. Children need time to play, and they need the opportunity without any obligation. Compulsory cricket is no substitute for imaginative games. Young children need to chase, and hide, and splash, and build camps, and climb trees, and pretend to be things that they are not. So do adolescents. If they are *organised* to do these things, however, the point is lost. They must have time to choose the kind of play they need. It is a stage of growing-up that can only be by-passed at a cost. Children who miss it become cautious, unsociable, inhibited or tense, and adults who have missed it may well try to win it back with unseasonable play throughout their lives.

The main adult reservation about play is that it is a waste of time: Work is the serious business of the day, and the more time you spend on it the better. For the children work *may* be the business of the day, but the important things are usually the ones that happen outside the classroom.

School is supposed to be a preparation for life, but on the whole all that the conventional school teaches you is how to cope with school, and preparation for life takes place outside the classroom, where you learn to make friends, choose values, accept the way other people react to you, find out who and what you like or dislike – in short, where you learn what sort of person you are. With young children this happens through play, and with adolescents it happens mainly through conversation. Just as the young need time to play, the adolescent needs time to talk.

It is in this play and this conversation that children learn from experience, learn from their own mistakes. Although children at the Middle School at Dartington are allowed to climb trees, to race bicycles in the copse, and to use the gym (though not its apparatus) unsupervised, there are worse accidents in activities supervised by adults than there are in free time. There seems to be a healthy natural caution in play that is lost when the responsibilty is taken by an adult in charge. My son may once have crashed painfully off a bicycle

Growth in independence is a vital part of the process
of growing up. Children who are given plenty of
independence may take risks, but in doing so they
learn their own limitations, and in fact they seldom
injure themselves.

ramp, but it is generally in P.E. lessons that limbs get broken.

Schools tend to disapprove of play because of the desperate need they feel to cram far too much into the first 16 or 18 years of a person's life. They make the extraordinary assumption that by the time you leave school you should be in some miraculous way ready for anything. It is as if the curriculum were expected to be infinite. To take a trifling example, you often hear complaints that children's spelling is not good nowadays. This usually means that a particular child's spelling is not good compared to adult spelling; usually this will be perfectly true. Adults who use the written word regularly presumably go on improving their spelling all their lives. If adults did not spell better than children there certainly would be something to worry about. If schools were not so intent on teaching the impossible – *all* spelling, *all* moral behaviour, *all* the A-Level syllabus – they would be able to give children more time for more important things.

This is not to suggest that conventional work done in a classroom cannot be valuable; it is only that we have got our sense of proportion wrong. It is more important to have a proper awareness of yourself and your place in the world than it is to be able to do quadratic equations. No one would quarrel with that. Yet we seem to think that schools should teach quadratic equations in every moment available, and the rest can be left to look after itself.

I imagine that we remember the most important events of our lives, and yet when you ask people for memories of their childhood, very few memories are concerned with lessons. Those that do come from the classroom are more likely to be about what happened than about what was being learnt. The experience of learning makes a stronger impression than the lesson itself. In the classroom what mattered was remembering the order of Henry VIII's wives; what matters when you look back is the humiliation of failure or the satisfaction of success, how you or some other child cheated, or the way you showed you didn't care by not even trying. These you still remember, but the names of the wives are uncertain now.

The Social Studies programme at Countesthorpe managed to transform the *subject* of study into the child's central concern because discovery is more interesting than instruction. It was from the children's central concerns that all investigation started – and I do not think they will ever forget this. I know of no other secondary school where this has been achieved.

THE SLOW ROAD TO MATURITY

The human being takes longer to mature than other living creatures. Foals are born able to run, whereas a human baby is incapable and defenceless. Animal mothers have usually lost interest in their offspring well before the next litter is born; human parents care for their young, by the same measurement, many times longer. It seems possible that this period of dependence and development may be one of the reasons for man's supremacy. Within the human race, the more civilised societies allow their young a longer time before they assume adult status, and within civilised societies people who have the longest training are usually the ones who are most respected. The advantage of a university career may well be the extra three years of time to play without adult responsibilities, rather than the actual knowledge acquired during those three years. A degree may be a help in getting a job in industry, but a first-class degree is sometimes thought to be a handicap.

The maturity that may come from a university education, if this theory is correct, is a piece of luck rather than a planned consequence. In schools, where children can be more easily controlled than university students, there is a curious twisting of the natural course of growth. Children are by law excluded from a number of adult activities, such as drinking, voting in elections and driving cars, but at school they are subject to social constraints and an academic narrowness that demand far more 'adult' behaviour than most adults would find acceptable. There is a great difference between decorum and industry enforced by discipline and decorum and industry that come naturally.

Children who go to universities from progressive schools are often rather scandalised at what seems to them to be infantile behaviour among the students. If you have spent the time you should have been playing bent over a classroom desk, you use your first opportunity to play when you should be doing some mature study. The progressive children's attitude is not one of pompous solemnity; it is just that they are able to get irresponsible playfulness out of their systems while still at

117

school. At an appropriate age adult standards come naturally as long as they haven't been enforced too soon.

To require children to take an interest in things before they can understand them, whether it be classical music or politics or Dickens, is to give them a totally false idea of the value of academic learning. To require them to behave with a dignity and courtesy that do not come naturally to them is to distort their sense of social values. The only practical way to develop good qualities in 10-year-olds or teenagers is not to require adult standards of them. There is a good, happy, right, helpful side to every age, and that is what we should encourage and rejoice in.

Morality and psychological health

It is obviously the function of schools to produce good adults. 'Good' may mean many different things – for instance 'having skills and knowledge that make you valuable to society' or 'conforming well to other people's image of adulthood'. The kind of goodness that concerns me in this chapter is *moral* goodness. It is hard to imagine that there is a school anywhere that does not intend to produce morally good people.

What do we mean by 'morally' good? Here again there are a number of different answers. 'Truly Christian,' you might reply, or 'possessed of all the virtues,' or 'having the right values.' It might be expected that progressive schools would have a different interpretation of the word from that of conventional schools, but the differences are only superficial.

It will be helpful to use the categories proposed by two American psychologists, R.F. Peck and R.J. Havighurst, who have published the results of intensive research into the moral development of children in a book entitled *The Psychology of Character Development* (New York, 1960). According to Peck and Havighurst there are five basic types of behaviour: *amoral, expedient, conformist, irrational-conscientious,* and *rational-altruistic.* A baby is supposed to be amoral – that is to say, without any moral understanding (not *immoral,* which means acting contrary to morality). The second stage is expedience: action taken in order to gain a reward, such as food or approval, or to avoid a penalty. Amorality and expedience, then, are the two childish stages; and Peck and Havighurst say that most adults reach – and are arrested at – stage three or four. In other words, they are either conformist or irrational-conscientious. The idea of conformity, of behaving in roughly

the same way as other people, is a familiar one; none of us likes to be laughed at, and few of us are bold enough to put forward new points of view unless we are fairly confident of at least some support. The term 'irrational-conscientious' needs some explanation.

Irrational-conscientious people have sets of rules to which they always adhere without questioning the reasons for them. These rules may be Pythagoras's decrees about not eating beans, not picking up what has fallen and not sitting on a quart measure, or they may be the Ten Commandments. They may be an unwritten code, such as the English class conventions, or the customs and privileges of any community. Where the conformist asks 'Is it expected?' the irrational-conscientious man asks 'Is it allowed?' He is ultimately obedient, and is at a loss if he can find no rule to obey.

Rational altruists have no need for rules. They are concerned for the welfare of other people, and they think carefully about the best ways of achieving this end.

In fact, of course, none of us falls completely into any of the categories, and our reasons for our actions are usually of several different kinds. I wear clothes, for instance, to keep warm, which is expedient, and because the law says I must, which is irrational-conscientious, and also because everybody else I know does; so I am conforming too. I may even be being rational-altruistic in wanting to spare other people the embarrassment of seeing me walk around with nothing on. When I buy a flag on a flag-day I may be altruistically thinking of other people – most probably the flag-seller, who looks anxious – but I am primarily obeying an irrational prompting from my conscience that says I must give to charity. I am also conforming, if most other people are buying flags.

It is not true, therefore, to say that the five types of behaviour are developmental stages. In *The Moral Development of Children*, a book published in England in 1970 (10 years later than *The Psychology of Character Development*), two British psychologists, Norman and Sheila Williams, point out that their research

Even in the free atmosphere of a progressive school there will be conformity in some things.

revealed responses of all types in the youngest children they questioned. Four-year-olds, they found, seemed capable 'of even the most "advanced" forms of moral thought', though expressed in simple ways. As you will remember, the altruistic response is generally regarded as chronologically the most advanced. But when asked why it's wrong to bully people, one 4-year-old answered, 'Cos it makes them cry.'

RATIONAL ALTRUISM ANALYSED

Few people would question the view that the rational-altruistic impulse is the highest. The only disagreement might come from people who maintain that moral issues are beyond human comprehension, that we must stick to rules revealed to us by God, whether they seem reasonable or not. This gives rise to some fine tragic situations, such as Abraham's preparations for the sacrifice of Isaac; but nowadays, though we can sympathise with Abraham's torment, few of us think he was right.

(One alarming thing about our own time is the tendency of some of the irrationally conscientious, bewildered by the decline of conventional religion, to cast around for new creeds and new codes of behaviour, and to accept the first guru who seems to them to speak with the voice of authority. We need to educate our children to be able to make judgements of their own.)

Most of us would agree, then, that the *moral* purpose of education is to create an environment in which rational altruism can best develop. The only alternative would be to try to teach our children to live gloriously selfish lives, accepting services and gifts from the benevolent rest of humanity. There would be two disadvantages to this alternative. One is that the 'benevolent rest of humanity', being by definition rational as well as altruistic, would soon start trying to make the selfish school leavers more useful to the world at large; the other, I believe, is that the desire to please others is an essential human characteristic, so that to live without any concern for others' feelings is unsatisfying. The only people likely to disagree with this position are those who believe that the quickest route to contentment is to take as much as possible for oneself without considering anyone else.

If it is agreed that from the point of view of every individual it is desirable to have the ability to behave rationally and

MORALITY AND PSYCHOLOGICAL HEALTH

altruistically, then anyone who does not wish to acquire this ability is mistaken. It may be that such a person has been merely misdirected by experience, as for instance in the case of sufferers from extreme poverty, but in the prosperous Western World it is more likely to be a matter of psychological maladjustment.

To put my proposition into simple words, a mentally healthy person wants to be good. This gives a new direction to the ideal of *mens sana in corpore sano*, which has generally been used only to justify the inclusion of football in school curriculums.

If you announce in the staff common room of a conventional school, 'A normal child wants to be good,' you are likely to attract criticism. 'Rubbish,' one critic may say. 'A normal child often wants to be naughty.' Part of the misunderstanding is due to the fact that though 'good' and 'naughty' are frequently used as opposites by people bringing up young children, they are not opposites in this instance: 'Good' meaning 'wise' and 'kind' is not the opposite of 'naughty' meaning 'disobedient'. Another part is due to the failure to recognise that it is possible to want two things at once, and a third to an illogical jump from the statement 'A normal child *wants* to be good' to the statement 'A normal child *is* good' (which is true), and then another jump to the statement 'A normal child is good all the time' (which is not true). It is of course also not true that a normal child is naughty all the time.

The least controversial way to say what normal children want is probably, 'All children want to be sensible.' And sensible behaviour in the moral sphere is rational altruism.

THE CASE AGAINST ORIGINAL SIN

It is a fundamental belief of progressive educationists that if you put children in the right environment, they will naturally tend towards altruism. This is in direct opposition to the idea of original sin and the feeling that if you don't tell children what is right and what is wrong they will never be able to find out. Unless you believe that rational altruism is an innate aspect of psychological health, the whole progressive system is obviously absurd.

The belief also implies its inverse, that irrational behaviour and selfish behaviour are signs of psychological disturbance. An analogy with physical health is useful here. Just as we all occasionally have colds and flu, so we all occasionally behave somewhat selfishly. Treatment is hardly necessary. But if we catch pneumonia or jaundice we need a doctor, and if we are kleptomaniac or manic depressive we need a psychiatrist. Broadly speaking, a healthy life-style and good diet are more important than medicines and are likely to make them unnecessary except for a person who is seriously ill. In the same way, a happy and supportive childhood is likely to promote psychological well-being except for the seriously disturbed.

Just as it is ridiculous to punish a child for catching a cold, so is it ridiculous to punish a child for lying. Colds and lying will persist, but there are better ways of dealing with them.

In the organization of most conventional schools there is an implied assumption that good behaviour is of no particular advantage to the individual. Such schools appear not to expect children to behave well unless good behaviour is reinforced by rewards, and bad behaviour is suppressed by punishments. This must mean that, in the opinion of the adults, without rewards and punishments the children would gain more from behaving badly than from behaving well. Progressive schools avoid rewards and punishments and rely on discussion and explanation, because in their philosophy the children them- selves stand to gain more by behaving well. We arrive once again at a circular definition: Good behaviour is that from which the children are likely to gain most benefit.

Some people really enjoy prize-givings. Awards and honours are handed out to children who have at best served the community, or more commonly just beaten everybody else at something. I can almost understand it. The honour sup- posedly gives the recipient a sense of merit, an awareness of recognition by others, an exaltation. It is a symbolic gesture of gratitude from the whole to a part. (Punishment, similarly, is a gesture of resentment from the whole to a part.)

I can *almost* understand it, but I still think prize-givings wrong. This is why:

In practice, prize-givings result in injustice. Not all the best people are rewarded, even in a limited sense of the word 'best'. More importantly, the kinds of behaviour that are rewarded are not the most important kinds of behaviour, but those that are most easily assessed, or possibly even those that are most easily marked. The implication of giving prizes for good work is that the prize is more important than the work – you work hard *in order to win a prize*. This removes all merit from the work itself, and distracts the child from any interest the work may have in itself. Prize-giving provides a motive for the expedient child, the conformist, and perhaps also for the irrational-conscientious (because you *ought* to strive to win prizes); but it actually hinders the development of altruism.

The implication of the whole society rewarding an individual is that the individual is separate from the society, or at least that the interests of the individual are in conflict with the interests of the group. That is another lesson that tends to suppress altruism. And finally, to the genuinely altruistic person, honour and disgrace are alike indifferent; if truly the best people have been found to win prizes, the prizes will not matter to them.

JUDGEMENT, NOT RULES!

In a conventional school the children have very little chance of making moral judgements. There are rules to govern their behaviour from the moment they enter the school gates in the morning until the moment they leave in the evening. There are rules about how they dress, how they speak, how they move, how they keep their books, where they sit, when they come and when they go. If they fight or play truant they are simply breaking rules. There may be lessons in religion or ethics, but in practice the moral decisions are all made by the adults in charge.

This is curious, because, just as in order to develop a healthy body you need to take physical exercise, so in order to develop healthy moral perceptions you have to take moral decisions. If you are told what to do all the time at school, you will not be able to direct yourself when you leave. You will have been trained vigorously as a conformist, as a follower of rules, and you will only survive as a healthy (i.e., normally rational) individual if you rebel, either openly or in the secret depths of your mind.

Neither the conformist nor the conscientious person presents a picture of mental health. The conformist may be confident and jolly as long as he knows how to behave, but is lost at once in unfamiliar surroundings. The conscientious person can

The girl with short hair won a local festival prize for recorder-playing in 1979; the very-different-looking girl won a prize for recorder-playing in 1984. They are the same girl. Does her hair style really matter?

become tense and anxious, wondering what ought to be done next. They are not able to show their true selves to the world, the one for fear of appearing strange, the other for fear of being wicked. Only rebels are able to act naturally, and if they have had the right experience they will have learned that in acting naturally *it is in their own interest to act morally.*

The gap between moral behaviour and conventional behaviour is actually emphasised in most schools. It is hard to believe that it can ever be morally wrong to wear red socks, or to have your ears pierced, or to help a friend with her work, or to laugh in the corridors, but these things are commonly treated as little less than crimes. The more unreasonable a rule, the severer the measures necessary to enforce it, it would seem, and so actions that actually inconvenience others, such as queue-barging or disturbing lessons, are often less severely punished than infringements of rules about uniform. This forces the school to present a very unbalanced set of values, and suggests to the children that all rules about behaviour are absurd.

Yet in a reasonably free environment it soon becomes obvious to children of any age that some rules about behaviour are necessary. The answer is that children should be invited to make the rules themselves – or at the very least to examine them critically. And if rules as a whole are to be respected, there should be none about things which don't really matter.

WHAT REALLY MATTERS

That raises another giant question: What really matters? Luckily the question can be cut down to size by adding two qualifications: What really matters that is likely to be ignored by children, and that can be regulated by making rules? Suddenly we are back with comparatively small things, such as bed-times and not borrowing people's bikes without asking. Nevertheless there is still a large area of disagreement, because for some people it is important for teachers to be called miss and sir, for teenage girls not to wear eye-shadow, for children not to get muddy and for every piece of written work to be written out first in rough and then copied out in neat. However, it is extremely unlikely that anyone who has been carried along by my argument as far as this would hold any of these views.

'What really matters?' is, in fact, a question that children like to ask themselves. The frontier flickers backwards and forwards, according to circumstances and personalities. At one time communication within the school will loom large, and at another safety rules for skate-boarding. On such issues discussion and the possibility of discussion among the children are more important than the details of final decisions. There are fundamental and important principles where discussion is unnecessary because everybody understands them. Schools do not need rules forbidding stealing and bullying, for instance. When such things occur, the children will discuss how to prevent them, perhaps, or whether a particular instance of teasing is really bullying or not, but no one questions the principles.

In a progressive school it is assumed that children will want to cooperate in a happy, smooth-running community. (The same assumption *may* be made in a strict and repressive school, but one implication of any system of punishment is that you do not expect children to want to cooperate.) They will not always know the best way of doing so, and in such cases they will need advice. They will also sometimes want to duck out of responsibilities, resist adult authority, or do something more interesting. All this is equally true of adults in any community.

Ordinary schools do not allow children the opportunity to learn how to deal with such choices; there is no choice. Progressive schools believe that by the very act of allowing children the opportunity to choose wrongly, you make it more likely that they will learn how to choose right.

I mentioned in an earlier chapter that in the school where I teach there are more broken limbs during activities supervised by adults than there are in the children's free play. This suggests, in physical terms, what I suggest is the case in moral terms: Children generally know how far they can go. Adults who assume responsibility for what goes on relieve the child of the need to make judgements as to what is either physically safe or morally wrong, and the result may well be broken arms in the gym and bullying by prefects.

THE DISCIPLINE OF SURROUNDINGS

One curious effect of a plethora of rules and adult dominance is that they remove children from the discipline of their sur-roundings. The reason children should not climb on roofs is that they may damage the roof, and they may fall off; it is not that they may get punished. The reason they have to go to bed by a certain time is that otherwise they will be too tired to work well the next day; it is not just that it is bed-time.

Rules in themselves do not constitute reasons; reasons dictate rules. Wherever possible children should be allowed to react to reasons, without the rules as an intermediary stage. Reasons are a consequence of reality. Rules are invented by teachers.

Where children are disciplined by reality rather than by teachers, the teachers are able to allow the children to be themselves. Children want to be sensible; all grown-ups have to do is to help them to understand how.

It is this respect for the position of the individual child that delights and astonishes so many newcomers to progressive schools. There is no mould into which every child is forced; everyone is free to choose an individual path. But just as adult control removes the discipline of reality, so freedom exposes you to it. Children actually welcome it, just as campers welcome the discipline of the elements, or climbers the discipline of the rock-face. It is not always pleasant, but it is utterly preferable to the artificial discipline of adult intervention. It is also extremely powerful. In spite of the absence of a mould, progressive-school children learn a true social responsibility that anxious mouldmakers are unable to emulate.

THEY LEARN TO BE GENTLE

The attitudes the children learn are, surprisingly, far more Christian than those learnt in most so-called Christian schools. 'Love thy neighbour as thyself' is the essence of rational altruism. The human products of gentle progressivism are far more likely to turn the other cheek than those of competitive conformity, and indeed one criticism of progressive education is that its products do not acquire sufficient cutting edge to get on with in the modern world. Cutting edge hardly seems a Christian virtue.

When I was teaching at Repton there were visiting preachers in chapel every Sunday, and one of them based his sermon on the text 'Go and sell that thou hast, and give to the poor'. 'This of course does not mean,' he explained, 'that we should sell all that we have and give the money to the poor.' At a progressive school both staff and pupils would be more likely to accept Christ's words at face value and admit to failing to live up to what he said. When people fear punishment, they lie to get out of it, and they bend the rules. If there is no punishment, they can safely admit to being in the wrong.

If you believe in original sin, it is obviously mad to allow people to admit to being in the wrong without getting punished. If, on the other hand, you believe that people want to do what is right, then it is mad to punish them for their mistakes. They need to be helped to understand the situation, not to be turned into enemies of society.

Even where there is no punishment, adults often seem to feel it necessary to humiliate children who have made mistakes. Humiliation by other people can never be anything but a harmful experience because of the apparent malice of the humiliator. Humiliation by events – which is perhaps another way of saying 'making mistakes' – though also a disagreeable experience, can be turned to advantage. Making mistakes is an all too common experience for children, and when they are so humiliated they need support rather than derision. With support they can form a clearer idea of what is and is not possible; without it they may only suffer a sense of failure. The ideal teacher helps children to achieve as much as they can while accepting without distress the limits of their abilities.

A good school, then, has few rules and no punishments. What is more, every child is treated with affection and respect, and so learns the essential self-confidence without which no genuinely independent choices can be made. Such a school will be filled with happy children. To be happy in such surroundings is a sign of mental health, which includes an attitude of rational altruism. So a good school is likely to produce good adults.

These good adults, however, will not appear 'good' to everybody. They will not willingly conform to customs they do not understand, they will probably put comfort before elegance, kindness before courtesy, and people before possessions, and though they will have a genuine respect for merit they will have no respect for rank. For all these reasons they will not fit easily into a convention-ridden society, and so may meet with disapproval. This does not seem to me to be to their discredit, but to the discredit of the disapproving society.

Each of us has a clear idea of what is good behaviour. The

reason we do not always behave kindly and well is that we are not sufficiently sure of being loved, admired and approved of if we do. Far too often we are afraid of being thought soft, unfair, foolish or unconventional. It takes security and self-confidence to override these fears. It is this security and self-confidence that schools should strive to develop. Only on such a firm basis can sincerely moral behaviour exist.

The search for truth

More than half a century ago Bertrand Russell wrote, 'The idea of speaking the truth to children is entirely novel; hardly anybody did it before the present generation.' I don't think he meant that people ever told lies about facts such as the names of the counties of England or the dates of English kings. What I think he meant was that the idea of *the importance of not telling lies to children* was 'entirely novel'. The stork, guardian angels, divine retribution for naughtiness, the absolute rectitude of all adults and the horrific consequences of masturbation were myths taught to children deliberately. Many superstitions and prejudices were handed on in good faith, but a lack of information about anything to do with sex and a plethora of false information about the consequences of misbehaviour were two areas of intentional deception.

In these two areas the situation is now very different. Information about sex is difficult to avoid, though unfortunately still difficult for adults to discuss with children. Young people often acquire bits of knowledge about intercourse or homosexuality long before they are able to digest them in any useful way, and the average parent is still as far as ever from guessing at a child's feelings and thoughts about sexuality. Memories of one's own childhood are no longer relevant, because the knowledge we used to have was so much more restricted. Society now seems to err on the side of too much information rather than too little; schools and parents are forced to struggle to set the provocative fragments acquired from magazines and television into some sort of coherent background.

Over the consequences of misbehaviour the pendulum has swung in the opposite direction. Instead of telling our children that if they tell lies they will never go to heaven, we give them no ethical advice at all. We allow them to believe that there are no consequences to lying beyond merely being caught out. In fact children know that the consequences are deeper, just as they knew they had sexual feelings before anyone would allow them to discuss them. Nowadays it is the ethical feelings that are passed over.

The search for ethical truths is a fundamental aim of progressive education, but before going on to elaborate this point I must pause to expand on what seems at first to be a rather less important issue, the search for factual truth.

It seems less important because there seems at first to be no problem. Teachers know factual truths, or at least we hope so, and they tell the children and try to make sure that they learn the facts. This attitude rides cheerfully over two difficulties. One is that the teachers may be wrong. The other is that to learn is not necessarily to understand – and to learn without understanding probably means soon to forget.

LEARNING THROUGH EXPERIENCE

Children, because of their lack of experience, cannot have a deep understanding of the world they live in. It serves little purpose for adults to do nothing but hand out information, even if the information is accurate. The child has a picture of the world and its workings that can be modified by information, but only too often the information offered to children is either irrelevant, or beneath them, or beyond them. What is needed is an opportunity for the child to test her picture of the world against reality, and then to make the necessary modifications herself.

If you happen to ask a question at a lecture, you remember your own question more clearly than anything the lecturer has said – more clearly even than his answer to your question. One of the odd things about conventional teaching is that it is usually the teacher who asks the questions and not the child. Only the child herself knows what she does not understand, what she needs explained, what she needs to know more about. It is the child who should be asking the questions.

At the same time the child needs experience (or information) to stimulate the questions. Suppose TV and newspapers have helped a boy form a picture of what it is like to be spastic, and he is interested; the next valuable step for him is to compare his picture with the reality, and adjust it until it fits with what he sees. He then hears or reads more, returns to reality again and makes further adjustments. Information is in a sense super-ficial; it is the experience, the deliberate, questioning experi-ence, that reshapes and improves the deep pictures in the mind. This results in learning that will last a lifetime, and that can be built on and retransformed.

This is emphatically not the sort of learning that usually goes on in schools. I remember a physics teacher demonstrating the expansion of metal under heat in a so-called 'experiment' which resulted in a metal rod being snapped. It was no more convincing than Uri Geller bending forks by psychic power. Children in this kind of situation are just told what the teacher wants them to know, and they learn it, if they learn it, with as little effort as possible. The children do not feel that they are in contact with important truths; they are learning to do tricks.

What they really want is to enlarge their limited picture of the world. They want to explore. They want to find out for themselves what is true. To sit in a classroom and listen to a teacher talking usually does little to satisfy this yearning.

A modern development in the teaching of sport illustrates what I consider an often wrong way to go about learning something. People used to play games. You learnt how to play well by playing. Nowadays there is a great deal of teaching of techniques, and it sometimes seems that many more children have lessons in tennis and memorise strokes than actually play the game.

Real learning has little to do with memorisation. In the ideal situation you would acquire an interest, perhaps from merely watching, and play a bit yourself; then, if keen enough, you would practise your strokes and service and take advice on how to improve your game. Then you would play more and find out what you still needed to improve, still needed to learn, still needed to practise. The process is endless, and it is a double one. You go from learning to reality, back and forth, back and forth, and you are always asking questions: 'How should I do this?' in one case, and 'Does it work?' in the other. They are questions which you personally want answers to; they are not the kind of questions teachers usually ask.

This committed and purposeful going back and forth is

absent from most school learning, particularly at the more advanced levels. You do social work *or* you study sociology. Yet a great part of the importance of children doing social work is that it should help them understand the implications of what they see, and sociology without reference to real people is like dry and rather unconvincing fiction.

One of the marvellous achievements at Countesthorpe was the staff's success at persuading their pupils to find topics of study of personal interest to them. Those teachers understood that children who choose their own topics will want to work at them, and will want to reflect on what they discover. There may be false starts, but in the end the interest will arise. Few children want to reflect on assigned subjects such as Norman castles or fashion through the ages, but they do want to reflect on their own discoveries, to test out the results of their reflections and to reflect on the consequences of the testing out. That is almost certainly the way adults learn to cope with their careers; why has not this truth been understood in schools?

It is the way scientists learn, and doctors learn, and musicians and artists and craftsmen and gardeners and cooks learn. It is also the way babies and young children learn. You collect information and you work with it and try it out, and you see what happens. You are not taught, except when you actively seek an explanation, and yet you learn and remember as you seldom learn and remember what you hear in a lecture or read in a book.

OUT IN THE FIELD

Dartington's 11-year-olds go for a week's camp every year. They live in individual tents in a rough field and cook their food on small open fires. They chop their wood, wash up their pots and pans, and share in chores for the benefit of the whole group. When it rains they have to try to keep their things dry. The rest of the time is occupied with exploration, walks, swimming, a survival exercise, games, songs and stories. For

Sport at a progressive school is not the religion that some schools make of it, but those who want to play still have the opportunity.

most of the children it is the most exciting experience of the year.

It provides a good example of the almost automatic learning that I am talking about. The children are given an opportunity which is organized by the staff. They explore it in various directions, sometimes under adult persuasion, sometimes because they feel like it, sometimes because they need to. What they learn is not a few facts but a whole new feeling about the world. Wind, hunger, cold, rain, sun, fire, food all appear in new guises.

Even at Dartington, however, classroom work is too often a struggle with the written page rather than a development of the understanding of reality. Because of its easy social relationships and interesting teachers, the school has usually had contented classrooms, but the teacher's role in the classroom is still thought of as being mainly to pass on information. Although the staff have always known that children who are trusted to choose their own standards of behaviour need only a small amount of adult encouragement to achieve a far deeper moral understanding than children who are strictly controlled, too few of us dare to believe the same is true of school work – that children trusted to choose their own subjects and style of study need only a small amount of adult encouragement to achieve a far deeper factual understanding than children under compulsion.

Countesthorpe, as I saw it, had taken this extra step with enormous success. The children chose their subjects of study and their approaches to those subjects. They discussed their choices carefully with their teachers, but the active pursuit of truth was their own. *They* worked with people, visited relevant places, did social work, interviewed, researched in archives and libraries and read books, newspapers and magazines. *They* went out into the world and made discoveries.

Campfire cooking is an exciting experience that gives 11-year-olds an opportunity for 'almost automatic learning'.

CHAPTER TEN

TEACHERS ALSO LEARN

Of course children allowed to discover truths for themselves may not discover the truths that adults expect. The adults then have to accept that their authority as adults has no particular meaning. The only real authority is the authority of truth, of things as they are.

This should be a delight to a teacher. One of the most enjoyable teaching experiences I've ever had was when my lesson was interrupted by children discovering that when you hold a pencil loosely, near one end, between finger and thumb, and shake it up and down, the pencil appears to bend. I abandoned the set lesson; instead the children and I together tried to discover what made this happen. We examined every hypothesis we could think of, including the possibility that the pencil actually did bend. In the end we found what we were all sure was the answer, though we were unable to prove it without a cine-camera. The delight of the experience for me was not the final discovery, but working with the children to solve a problem that I myself did not know the answer to.

The introduction of computers into schools has given many teachers a similar experience. Children often know more about programming than adults, and so the teachers have found themselves in the delightful position of learning from the children, and perhaps learning *with* them, instead of just setting work and letting the children do all the learning.

These are comparatively trivial examples, but they illustrate the idea that a search for understanding is more important than the impassive handing on of information. In his lectures on the foundations of mathematics the Viennese philosopher Ludwig Wittgenstein made a similar point. 'I am trying to conduct you on tours of a certain country,' he said. 'I will try to show that the philosophical difficulties which arise in mathematics as elsewhere arise because we find ourselves in a strange town and do not know our way. So we must learn the topography by going from one place in the town to another, and from there to another, and so on. And one must do this so often that one knows one's way, either immediately or soon after looking around a bit, wherever one may be set down.' (From *Remarks on the Foundations of Mathematics*, translated from the German by G.E.M. Anscombe, Blackwell, 1978.)

The teacher's role must be first to find out where the child is starting. No two children will start from the same place. They will want to explore their immediate surroundings. It is essential to allow them to explore, and not merely to show them a map; even if they understand the map it will not show them colours of buildings and landscape, people and animals, or changes in the weather. Far too much of education has consisted of learning maps by heart before you have even learnt map-reading. This is perhaps to learn what is true, but it is not to learn the truth. It is like learning history in a language that you cannot understand: Although you can reel off long sections of it, the knowledge is of no value to you.

MORAL GUIDANCE

In ethical and social education the issues are very much the same. It is necessary to start from the position and understanding of each individual child, to help that child find her own way around. And, to echo Wittgenstein, one must do this so often that the children know their way, either immediately or soon after looking around a bit, wherever they may be set down.

It is important to avoid using children as symbols or putting them into situations they cannot understand. Some children love to be pages or bridesmaids because to be near the centre of attention is perhaps delightful. But many are bewildered or distressed by being placed in a situation which means nothing to them and where there are no guidelines for behaviour except blind obedience. The sentimental smiles with which people admire a small boy presenting a posy to a celebrity are caused by an emotion which the child himself would find offensive in the extreme. There is a Botticelli Madonna who is surrounded by angels with boys' faces, and all the faces are despairingly bored, as presumably the models themselves were when Botticelli painted their portraits.

The only lesson a child can learn from such situations is that it is acceptable to take part in a ritual one does not understand. This on the one hand condones (or even recommends) insincerity; on the other hand it lays people of any age open to dangerous commitment. You might find yourself participating in a human sacrifice when you thought you had just gone to church.

That may be a foolish exaggeration, but some people's unfortunate habit of unquestioningly joining action groups, clubs, religious societies and encounter groups often results in

141

them finding themselves taking part in things that they would never consider doing as individuals.

Children cannot be expected to detect truth or falsehood, rightness or wrongness, in situations they do not understand. On the other hand they tend to be extremely interested in discussing such issues when the situation is within their mental grasp. There are few issues that children will debate with more passion than the issues of justice.

Faced with this enthusiasm, it is curious that so many teachers fall back on rules and commands rather than helping children to develop their moral sense by wrestling with real ethical problems. Adult opinions are dealt out as if they were facts; there is no question of discussion. Yet in this sphere, even more clearly than in the sphere of computing which I cited earlier, it cannot be true that adults have the whole truth and are therefore right to hand it out to children from their pulpits. The adults too are searching.

I am afraid that too many teachers assert their authority because they are not confident that the real world will justify their assertions. The only possible justification for any moral assertion is that it is right. Children are not idiots. If it is true that learning is a pleasure, then children will learn; if it is true that peace and justice are important, then children will strive for them. They will strive for them, that is, with the right encouragement, and as long as they feel they are being taken seriously. If they are treated as idiots who cannot decide on proper ways of behaviour for themselves, then it may be that they will react like idiots. It is very difficult to learn from someone who is saying to you, by implication, 'All these matters are beyond you, so there is no point in trying to understand.'

A child's sense of moral outrage, for instance over the mistreatment of an animal, is likely to be far stronger than an adult's. Perhaps the adult feels wearily that there are more important issues and that the child's distress is merely irritating, but it is strange that we tend to make little of the emotions instead of trying to discuss the situation and perhaps help the child to extend his area of sympathy. The adult may have become less sensitive largely out of self-protection, because one cannot live permanently lacerated by moral indignation (as with adult knowledge of the world perhaps one ought to be). However, that does not mean that the child is wrong or silly.

Outrage about nuclear weapons is stronger among the young than among the middle-aged. Yet the middle-aged still reproach the young with having no moral values.

EIGHT NEW COMMANDMENTS

A few years ago, after several lessons concerning the Ten Commandments and their shortcomings, a 13-year-old progressive-school girl produced the following astonishing list of truly important commandments:

Love your work.
Look happy at your past, and look for your future.
Never let yourself down.
Never accuse when you're not sure.
Think positive.
Help anyone who needs it.
Enjoy yourself, but don't hurt other people while you do.
You are not forced to do things, but do them when they are needed.

Those eight commandments seem to me to reflect the extraordinary moral vigour of their originator. Children, when given the chance, are deeply concerned about right and wrong. What schools ought to do is to allow them to experience ethical dilemmas, to help them to find their way, to help them to arrive at true values through their own experience so that they know true values, understand them and feel them as part of themselves. For a child a moral precept such as 'Thou shall not commit adultery' might as well be written in Swahili.

The experiences of a child of divorcing parents will engrave themselves on his mind forever. Schools need to help children to use such knowledge to create their own ethics, and not to lapse merely into despairing cynicism. The truth can be a demanding and cruel teacher, but its lessons are the only lessons that need to be learned. Luckily, these are also the lessons that people most want to learn. The search for truth is a fundamental human instinct, and it ought also to be a fundamental objective of education. It is vastly more important than such commonly accepted objectives as order, good manners and ethical conformity.

I want to make one last point about the search for truth, particularly as it affects any progressive school as a whole. In a progressive environment the staff and pupils together search for the best possible way to run their school. They have no dogma to contend with, only a history which tells them what has worked pretty well in the past. They are – or ought to be – unusually open-minded and ready to try out new ideas. They are, after all, seeking the truth, and very few of them will believe that they have already discovered it in its entirety. So they try out new ideas, and with as much sincerity and detachment as they can muster, they see whether they work. If they work they are adopted; if they don't work the school can revert to the way it was running before – which was, after all, as good a way as the assembled community could devise.

Such a totally pragmatic approach may come as a surprise to those who regard progressives as sentimental idealists out of touch with the real world. In fact, though, it is people with systems and doctrines who are driven, by those very systems and doctrines, to ignore the real world in order to assert that they are right.

THE PROGRESSIVE PRESENCE

A truly progressive school, then, cannot go wrong for long; as soon as reality shows that some policy is mistaken, the policy can be changed. This results in a mood of self-confidence among staff and pupils because they are aware that their opinions count, that they are part of a whole that they themselves can always adjust in order to come closer to the unattainable ideal. High aims are often obscured by mundane problems, but the existence of these high aims is understood by everyone. However much people in progressive education may differ on superficial issues, no one doubts the importance of the search for truth.

Any child who has been at a progressive school for more than a year or two acquires a particular kind of presence

In a progressive atmosphere the staff and pupils together are encouraged to search for the best possible way to run their school.

seldom acquired elsewhere. It owes something to self-confidence and something to modesty; people who have been through such schools have nothing specifically in common but this presence. They may be quiet or assertive, elegant or casual, acquisitive or prodigal, but they are all solid personalities, unafraid to be themselves. They are nonconformists in that they conform consistently only to their own characters and are not one thing in one society and something else elsewhere.

This is not to say that they are insensitive to or disruptive of other people's customs. If they find themselves in what seems to them an unreasonable society they feel no need to impose their opinions on other people. It is as if they have learnt and accepted the truth about themselves, and do not need to act as if they had qualities they have not. If they have not yet learnt the *whole* truth about themselves, they are not afraid to learn it. They know that the dignity of being a person is enough, and there is no need to strive to be an important person. It is partly the fidgetty striving and social jostling that makes other people undignified by comparison.

A child who has grown up through a progressive school would never actually say, 'Here I am, such as I am. You may like me or dislike me, but unless I accept your reasons you will not make me change.' But that is somehow the implication of such a person's bearing, and it has a quality about it that is more important than charm or magnetism, although it often embraces them. In so far as it is possible to say that people can be true to themselves, this quality is very close to truth.

Absence of dogma

'If tolerance and respect for weakness and horror of force and oppression and this fumbling attempt to put sensitivity and the heart above all the twists of logic, above all the decrees of ideologies – if all that were only a doctrine, a philosophy, one more system in our way, I would have let those colours die out of my sky a thousand times rather than see so many of my comrades give their lives for them.

It is not ideas alone that I stand for.'

(From *The Colours of the Day*, by Romain Gary)

In some ways it is very comfortable to stand for ideas alone. It is much easier to argue about ideas than it is to argue about feelings, and if the system is sufficiently authoritarian you don't even have to argue. One boy who left a progressive school to go into the army said he found it a marvellous change because at last he did not have to make decisions. It is easier not to have to think.

Progressive schools do not allow this ease to either staff or pupils. Everyone is required to think. There are no received opinions to fall back on. There are so few rules that you have to make continual decisions as to what you will do. As soon as you arrive you must begin to use your own judgement and discover your own personal pattern of behaviour.

New staff sometimes find this difficult. Not only is there no system of punishment to support the teachers; they do not even get told how to handle a situation without it. There is no clear pattern for them to fall in with, and failures are personal failures with the children, not impersonal failures with the system. They are expected to have confidence in their own judgement, and their judgement has to be based on accurate perceptions.

Some people who teach well in orthodox schools cannot adjust to progressive schools. I mentioned earlier the P.E. teacher who preferred to take a job in a comprehensive school where children did not 'ask so many questions'. It will not work if a teacher in a progressive school condescends to pupils, or tries to require adherence to unreasonable regulations, or treats his own subject with disdainful flippancy, or assumes that there is no need to prepare lessons, or simply shows himself to be unworthy of the children's affection and respect.

Most of the criteria for good teaching are the same at a progressive school as they are anywhere else: clarity, enthusiasm, organisation, conscientiousness and so on. But others are very different. I myself am an example of a teacher who can manage in a progressive atmosphere but am useless in a conventional school. My excuse is that in an environment where children are accustomed to control by personal domination of the teachers they cannot adjust to an occasional lesson with a teacher who prefers to rely on the authority of circumstances. 'Look,' I remember saying, 'you must be quiet in the front or the people at the back won't be able to hear what I am saying.' To children who were used to being clouted this sort of approach was absurd.

New children at progressive schools, unlike some new teachers, are nearly always delighted with the atmosphere. From the point of view of the school they may take some time to settle, but from their own points of view there are usually no problems. Occasionally, however, things go wrong. Here is a fictitious account from a novel written for children by C.S. Lewis, whose hostility to what he calls Experiment House is perhaps based on an account provided by someone who had once hated being a pupil at a progressive school:

'It was a dull autumn day and Jill Pole was crying behind the gym. She was crying because they had been bullying her. This is not going to be a school story, so I shall say as little as possible about Jill's school, which is not a pleasant subject. It was "co-educational", a school for both boys and girls, what used to be called a "mixed" school; some said it was not nearly so mixed as the minds of the people who ran it. These people had the idea that boys and girls should be allowed to do what they liked. And unfortunately what ten or fifteen of the biggest boys and girls liked best was bullying the others. All sorts of things, horrid things, went on which at an ordinary school would have been found out and stopped in half a term; but at this school they weren't. Or even if they were, the people who did them were not expelled or punished. The Head said they were interesting psychological cases and sent for them and talked to them for hours. And if you knew the right sort of things to say to the Head the main result was that you became a favourite rather than otherwise.'

In fact there is certainly less bullying and less crying behind the gym at progressive schools than in most others; in reality poor Jill's problems would have been more likely to be homesickness and a consequent inability to decide how to 'do what she liked'. In a conventional school routine, compulsory games and organised free time would perhaps have helped her.

In *The Silver Chair*, the 1953 book from which the above extract is taken, Jill is redeemed by meeting Aslan, a Christ-like lion who rules over the kingdom of Narnia. Aslan is ultimate authority. After Jill and her fellow-pupil Eustace have been through heroic adventures, Aslan bears them back to Experiment House, along with a prince called Caspian, and this is what happens:

'At the same moment Jill saw figures whom she knew only too well running up through the laurels towards them. Most of the gang were there – Adela Pennyfather and Cholmondely Major, Edith Winterblott, "Spotty" Sorner, big Bannister and the two loathsome Garrett twins. But suddenly they stopped. Their faces changed, and all the meanness, conceit, cruelty and sneakishness almost disappeared in one single expression of terror. For they saw the wall fallen down, and a lion as large as a young elephant lying in the gap, and three figures in glittering clothes and weapons in their hands rushing down upon them. For, with the strength of Aslan in them, Jill plied her crop on the girls and Caspian and Eustace plied the flats of their swords on the boys so well that in two minutes all the bullies were running like mad, crying out, "Murder! Fascists! Lions! It isn't *fair*." And then the Head (who was, by the way, a woman) came running out to see what was happening.'

The phrase I want to draw attention to is 'With the strength of Aslan in them'. In the view of a committed Christian like C.S. Lewis the strength of the individual is not enough; it is the power of supernatural authority that we need. With this power we are able to return evil for evil, to smite our enemies with riding crops and the flats of our swords and have no feeling of responsibility or guilt. It is a curiously Old Testament view.

C.S. Lewis was certain that children needed dogmatic authority and discipline in order to be contented, and he was quite right in assuming that Experiment House would disagree with him. But he grossly misrepresented any real-life Experiment House, which children I have spoken to have seldom identified with their own school.

Broadly speaking, in spite of Lewis's views, progressive-school children are happy with an established framework to the day, plus the chance to fill in gaps as seems best to them. Some teachers, however, are the products of very different systems of education, and they long for firmer guidance. Their attitude is understandable.

When all children are different and you have no rules to govern your dealings with them, you have to handle each child differently. Since teachers are all different too, there can be no universal approach. New teachers arriving at progressive schools are often not even given a syllabus to teach. There will be time-tabled lessons and the previous teacher's books to choose from; the newcomer will be expected to select whatever suits her best, and to teach what she thinks appropriate in her own particular way. If that doesn't seem appropriate in practice she must try something else. It is not an easy task.

The absence of dogma about the best way to teach is valuable for everyone concerned, however. Just as the child is the best judge of how he should learn, so is a teacher the best judge of how she should teach. To allow teachers as much latitude as possible is to give them the chance to develop their teaching talents to the limit. Teachers can help each other by suggestions and comments, but no one lays down the way things have to go.

WHEN 'NO DOGMA' BECOMES DOGMA

Countesthorpe appeared to be an exception to this rule. The view that individual learning is *always* better than group teaching seemed to me to be dogmatically imposed, and what is more I saw it imposed in situations where it did not really work. In the pod I visited, maths seemed just as unpopular as it ever is elsewhere. In order to make sure that children could work independently at their own pace, the teaching was done through a system of work cards. Now of course work cards, though they can be tackled individually, dictate the course of learning every bit as conclusively as a textbook, and in the ideal world each child would approach maths by a different route. Group teaching seemed to have been avoided without anything more valuable being put in its place; the system of individual work cards meant that the children missed the stimulation that sometimes comes from working together. When a subject is as dry as maths is for most pupils, the social interaction of a classroom can help to make it more interesting.

Science also seemed to be unsuitable for individual learning, though for different reasons. Because of the complexity of scientific equipment it is usually not possible to set up everyone's experiments in the space and time available. And because of the enormous extent of allegedly necessary scientific knowledge, children have to be guided fairly rapidly along recognised paths if they are to get at all far.

This is not to say that autonomous learning may not in fact be a good way of tackling maths and science. The tasks I saw the Countesthorpe children doing in maths were not self-selected; perhaps if some way had been found of persuading them to select relevant mathematical tasks, the situation would have been ideal. In science it may be more important to learn to devise experiments to test your own theories than to acquire the vast vocabulary of chemical and biological terms that seems to constitute the bulk of the examination syllabus. Nevertheless, the proposition that individual learning is always better than group teaching was certainly not being demonstrated in these cases, and it seemed to me that the approach was being demanded for theoretical reasons from people who were not themselves happy with it.

There is an enormous difference between saying 'This is the approach you must use' and 'I *think* this is the best approach.'

In the second case you are being asked to contribute to the discussion, whereas in the first you are merely being told what to do – and the instructions may, after all, be wrong.

To assert that there should be no dogma, either for children or staff, may also appear to be dogmatic. What is more, unless the whole difference of atmosphere between progressive and orthodox schools stems from this one tenet, it seems likely that the word 'progressive' implies additional hidden dogma. 'There shall be no punishment' is a probable candidate as an imposed commandment, as is 'Thou shalt not set thyself above the child'. Such tenets, however, are pragmatic rather than dogmatic. They can be recast in such forms as 'It usually seems best not to impose teachers' convictions upon pupils' or 'Generally speaking we find that punishment achieves little, and as it appears to be an evil in itself it is better to avoid it'.

EXCEPTIONS TO ALL 'RULES'

Tom Larssen, a huge man who used to teach P.E. at Dartington, once lost his temper with a boy and knocked him down. Tom, who had not been long at the school, went to tell the head, Bill Curry, what he had done, fully expecting to be sacked. 'Who was it?' said Curry. Tom told him. 'Oh, good,' said Curry. 'It was about time someone knocked him down.'

This is enough to show that progressive schools do not adhere to any dogma about their basic philosophy. It follows that religious dogma must also be open to question. There will be no denial, but also no assertion. There are often committed Christian staff members who are active members of their churches; they may tell the children what they believe, but the children will not accept any assertions as to the truth of these beliefs. Religious faith is a personal matter.

All this is part of a modern trend which I optimistically

Many people mistakenly suppose that progressive educators banish classrooms from their schools. On the contrary, much of the instruction is surprisingly conventional. Classrooms may be informal and cheerful, as here, but the lessons are orderly and effective.

believe to be widespread outside the world of education: a general denial of the importance of authority, and its replacement by individual responsibility. The trend seems to have developed since the war, and to be commoner among the young than the old. Adolescents are at an age when one of the main purposes of life is to establish one's own identity, to prove that one is responsible for one's actions. Adults have often given up the idea and fallen back on some form of determinism, either to excuse their irresponsible behaviour or out of sheer despair. Young people who want to change the world are regarded as merely Quixotic.

A small illustration of the sort of change I mean is the change in the results of a psychological experiment first carried out 15 or 20 years ago, and then again more recently. Subjects were invited in groups into a room where there were headsets of earphones and microphones. They put these on and heard two tones, one of which plainly went on for longer than the other. They were then supposed to say which tone, the first or the second, had lasted for the longer time. In fact, also recorded on the tapes after the two tones were a number of different voices giving the wrong answer. Subjects naturally assumed that they were hearing the voices of other people in the room, and in the original experiment most of them chimed in with the apparent majority opinion. The 1980s subjects stuck to their own right answers.

What other people did – and in particular what other people of the same social class did – used to be the proper thing for *you* to do, and to do the proper thing was right and good and the purpose of life. People wore class-revealing uniforms such as city suits, print frocks, collarless shirts, expensive hats. It was reprehensible to step out of line even slightly – by, for instance, wearing a brown suit in the Stock Exchange. When you spoke to a person (or ignored people), you spoke to or ignored them as a class, not as individuals.

It is still true that in most cases a waiter is simply a waiter and not a potential friend who happens to be working in a restaurant. And a shop assistant is simply a shop assistant, the customer a customer, and there is still little chance of potential friendship or personal involvement between them. Nevertheless the distinction is much less sharp than it used to be, as is shown by the modern informality of dress and behaviour in almost all social contact.

In 1956 a young man named Trevor Williams, having just gone down from Cambridge, was in his first job in a solicitor's office in London. He wrote an article for the university magazine *Granta* describing his efforts to make an impression. Here are a few excerpts from the article:

'Everywhere I am treated with deference, my quips are smiled at without rancour, my haste and tardiness are overlooked, and yet somehow they have it over me. Why am I so like a boy at his first dance?

'Disconsolate, I tackle this question over the teapots of a spinsters' refuge in Holborn, and attempt to pinpoint that particular defect in me which makes the ordinary relationships of everyday business such a gooseflesh experience. And then it dawns. "The ordinary relationships of everyday business," that's the clue. They don't give a damn, these secretaries, these solicitors, these directors. Here I've been trying to establish contact, sweating to bring them within the great circumference of my affection, and they don't give a damn. All they care is that the business should be done as smoothly as possible. Good manners are recognised as an important tool in effecting this end, but as for caring whether I am gay or gawky, shy or resolute, man or woman, why, they don't even notice. So that's that. From now on I shall be controlled, distant and imperturbable by the simple process of not giving a damn.'

As he walks away from the café, the article continues, young Williams manages to sink into what seems to him to be the right mood:

'I sense nothing but the rhythm of the walking and the gentle kaleidoscope of unknown faces that is the changeless background of a London walk, a myriad faces bobbing, wafting, disappearing, glinting straight into the line of vision, like the reflections of the evening sun upon a rippling lake viewed by a traveller from the stern of an eastbound ship, a traveller who gazes into the water saying to himself from time to time: "How beautiful the sun is on the lake," but whose thoughts are far away.'

He is suddenly reminded of his time at Cambridge, 'and for a moment as unguarded as when one sees a long-forgotten friend on a passing bus, I feel a wave of longing for the days when travellers in their scores would have jumped into the sunlit lake to re-arrange the glinting ripples.'

Nowadays I think many more people are prepared to jump in. Many more people are coming to accept the idea of personal responsibility for whatever they do and to reject the idea that without dogma there will be chaos, that the basis of morality is conformity. Instead of conforming, they believe, you should do what you yourself feel to be right. That attitude is what produced the hippies, and the ecologists, and Oxfam and the feminists.

Not all such excursions into self-direction are successful, as is shown by the fate of the hippies. Many fringe people, after a brave try at doing without authority, fall back on fringe religion for their framework. It is not easy to accept responsibility for your own behaviour. Nevertheless, the trend towards individual responsibility exists; and unless they have been actively taught otherwise, most young people are eager for it, even though they may have had little practice in the true exercise of free choice.

Progressive schools exist in order to teach children to choose. And their methods are based on undogmatic precepts such as those in the following list of cautious suggestions (beginning with two I have already made):

It usually seems best not to impose teachers' convictions upon pupils.

Generally speaking we find that punishment achieves little, and as it appears to be an evil in itself, we prefer to avoid it.

Children seem to assimilate more when they are interested than when they are under compulsion. Even so, they are likely to accept the necessity of learning some dry information and to be glad of adult insistence on its being learnt.

Lots of us think that teachers should help children to acquire information, but should never merely inform them. As the Paris progressive school 'La Source' puts it: 'Le professeur n'enseigne plus . . . . il cherche avec l'élève.'

Affection seems a better starting-point for moral education than authority.

Most children consider fairness to be an important issue. They enjoy arguing about it, and usually arrive at just conclusions even though they may have started merely from a wish to improve their own position.

Some form of routine seems a necessary part of anyone's life, but we also need times when we can choose what to do.

People are likely to respond better to rules and regulations if they have made them themselves, and if it is clear that they are made for the benefit of the community as a whole.

Happy children are more often kind, friendly, honest and conscientious than unhappy children.

However benevolent, a regime under the control of one group is unlikely to be ideal for the group or groups being controlled. This is as true when the groups are adults and children as it is when they are social classes.

There often seem to be cases where the individual is an exception.

All these precepts bear some relationship to the following statement of my personal reasons for believing the progressive system to be the only proper way of educating children:

It is part of human nature to want to be good. Our moments of malice are failures. We are sometimes mistaken as to the nature of goodness.

It is also part of human nature to resist force. To try to force children to be good is counterproductive. Since children want to be good anyway, it is unnecessary.

Obedience is no part of goodness. Unless the reasons for right behaviour are discovered within ourselves, we will not behave rightly when there is no compulsion.

The teacher's role is to help children to develop their own sense of what is right. When a child is loved and respected, and has proper experience of the discipline of reality, this personal sense is likely to flourish. Unreasoning discipline imposed by other people is likely to inhibit it. So is determined adherence to any dogmatic creed.

Romain Gary, quoted at the head of this chapter, was talking of the horrors of the Second World War, and for him 'sensitivity and the heart' were at least symbolised, if not represented, by a love affair. Progressive education is also a 'fumbling attempt to put sensitivity and the heart above all the twists of logic, above all the decrees of ideologies.' It is not ideas alone that we stand for.

What is it all for?

'It is said that a pupil, after listening to a demonstration, asked what he would gain by learning geometry, whereupon Euclid called a slave and said, "Give the young man three-pence, since he must needs make a gain of what he learns." '
(From Bertrand Russell's *History of Western Philosophy*)

Euclid knew that learning was a delight in itself and despised anyone who wanted more than pleasure from it. This is a view that was sadly forgotten when teachers felt they had to beat children to make them learn, and so taught them that learning was second only to being beaten in its unpleasantness.

Things have improved slightly, but a common modern view is that learning is only valuable if it leads to a job – the equivalent of the three-pence that Euclid's slave handed out. Schools are supposed to turn children into employable adults, and at as high a level as possible. It is considered better to turn out doctors and managers than nurses and workers. What you need to do to improve your prospects is to pass exams. Whether or not you can pass exams, it is essential to dress conventionally and conduct yourself with decorum.

The accepted image of an ideal school-leaver is of a healthy-looking, demure young woman in a summer dress, with books under her arm, walking into her new university. You see her in advertisements for banks. Or perhaps the school-leaver is pictured as a healthy-looking, demure young man in an open-necked shirt, jersey and trousers (not jeans). Although the picture might please a conservative public who did not know the students, neither the schools that educated them nor their parents nor the students themselves would feel that it is true to

life. Conventionality and a university place are not the sole aims of education for anybody.

A.S. Neill wanted above all things that Summerhill children should be happy. This seemed to me, with its implications of fulfilment and peace of mind, to be an excellent objective, until my first wife, Jenny, who had been educated at a progressive school, said that she wanted our children to be above all kind. It is, I believe, difficult to be kind without being happy, and it is unusual to be happy without being kind, but kindness is the more important goal. What is more, there are circumstances in which happiness is impossible, but it is never impossible to be kind.

These two objectives, it should be noted, are not incompatible with the conventional image of a university student. They are possible objectives for everyone – the conformist and the rebel, the athlete and the cripple, the genius and the dunce.

With such considerations in mind, I want to discuss a number of objectives that schools do, or have in the past, set themselves. In discussing the objectives I shall be reiterating many points from earlier chapters with the intention mainly of supporting my view that whenever progressive and conventional schools agree on an objective, it is the progressive schools that have found the more rational method of achieving it. For that reason the following pages can stand as both a summary of and a conclusion to this book.

PURPOSES OF EDUCATION

1. Status

Education undeniably gives status. I would like to think it a consequence rather than a purpose, but I am afraid that in many people's minds status is a major objective.

The desire to buy status is one of the reasons people send

A.S. Neill said that above all things he wanted his pupils to be happy. This might seem at first sight to be a self-centred ideal, but it ceases to seem so when you realise that children need each other in order to be themselves.

their children to public schools. I start my list with it because this book started with my experience of teaching at a public school.

To value education primarily as a source of status is of course utterly philistine. It is not an objective of any progressive school.

2. *Preparation for life*

The notion that education is preparation for life implies that children are not fully alive. Leaving school, it suggests, is like being born again, a butterfly emerging from a chrysalis.

In fact, leaving school is probably less important than moving house, changing your job, getting married, having children, suffering bereavement or plenty of other experiences. School is part of life, and the more it is regarded as being of value in itself, as opposed to merely the preparation for something more important, the better.

I think the preparation-for-life notion stems from a fear that unless children are taught the right things at school they will never be able to work in factories, or look after livestock, or keep accounts or whatever their jobs may be. In fact, apart from reading, writing and arithmetic in some occupations, almost all you need to know about any job is either taught to you when you get there or acquired from experience. Most of what you have learnt at school is completely irrelevant.

Anyone who has gone on to a university course in science will remember being told to forget everything they had been taught before. I did a course in elementary bookkeeping before I went to work in an office; in the course I had learnt about profit-and-loss accounts and balance sheets, but in the office I copied figures from statements into ledgers and added them up. Most jobs can be explained on site in a few minutes. Where special training is needed, most employers provide it, either by a specific apprenticeship or training scheme or by starting young people off as assistants to experienced people.

Perhaps preparation for life means spending time learning how to type, how to program computers, how to weld, how to cook. All these seem to me to be valuable skills for people who need them. However, if you haven't learnt them by the time you leave school, you can quickly learn them afterwards. It would be a shame to limit all education to the teaching of practical skills. The fact that a skill is 'practical' does not automatically make it useful.

When my first child was 2 or 3 years old I remember comparing her behaviour with that of the 12-year-olds I was working with and wondering how on earth we were going to teach her the mature behaviour that these children showed. Of course by the time she was 12 she had learnt it without being taught. Children don't have to be taught how to grow up. They cannot be prevented from doing so. Similarly, a school does not need to prepare children for life. They prepare themselves.

If school is thought of as preparation for something else, it has no value in itself; it becomes valuable only when finished, and childhood becomes a succession of rehearsals with no performance. This view seems to me patronising and ridiculous; children probably get more out of life than adults. What you should do at school is not prepare for life, but live.

3. The instilling of a particular set of values
As Rudyard Kipling showed in *Stalky & Co.*, a school cannot instil a set of values merely by preaching it. The lack of true Christian values among people who have been prayed with every morning of their school lives is good evidence of this.

Luckily it doesn't matter. Children have values of their own, and what is important is giving them the opportunity to develop and refine their understanding rather than trying to compel them to accept somebody else's particular doctrine.

4. Ability to make constructive use of leisure
This newcomer to the list of educational objectives has made its appearance since the work began to run out. It is no good educating people for work if there isn't going to be any for them; so you have to think of alternatives.

Just as I don't believe people should be educated for work, so I cannot see that they should be educated for leisure.

Let me quote a passage from *On Britain*, a book by Ralf Dahrendorf, former Director of the London School of Economics (published by the B.B.C. in 1982):

'Work is human action that is heteronomous, imposed by external needs, be they needs of survival or of power. Activity, on the other hand, is human action which is freely chosen, which offers opportunities for self-expression, which carries its satisfaction within itself, which is autonomous . . . [This difference] enables us to make sense of the fact that while our societies are running out of jobs, they are certainly not running out of work in the conventional sense. There is enough to do, enough also for people's self-respect and to give meaning to their lives . . . It may well be that people do not prefer leisure, but that they prefer activity. Their self-respect is quite often determined by achievements other than those of their job.'

There is no need to educate people to make constructive use of leisure. What we all need to know is how to make constructive use of time.

5. Excellence
Lots of schools claim to run in pursuit of excellence. In spite of its vagueness this purpose seems fine to me as long as it does not involve ignoring or condemning the merely good, the mediocre and the feeble. Most of us will never excel at anything, but that does not mean that all our efforts are a waste of time. As G.K. Chesterton said, 'If a thing is worth doing it is worth doing badly.'

Excellence as an objective often goes in tandem with success. Without more context, 'success' is a vague word that can be defined in different ways. If it means, as it often does, doing better than most other people, then it follows automatically that most people cannot achieve success. If it means managing to do whatever you set out to do, then it seems to be more a matter of matching your aims to your abilities than a definition of an abstract standard of achievement.

In preference to excellence and success as objectives, I would like to see personal *involvement*; only a few can excel, but everyone can become involved. Countesthorpe shows that the pursuit of personal involvement can even produce better work than the pursuit of excellence; as so often, the progressive way, in spite of appearing to ignore conventional aims, actually achieves some of them more effectively than conventional methods.

6. Leadership
Leadership, a much-derided objective of the old public schools, no longer seems to be regarded as important. The public

schools tried to turn every boy into a leader, regardless of his character. He was to go out into the colonies and command men, or stay at home and run an estate or an industry. As he grew up through the school, every boy who was considered in the least dependable came in the end to a position of authority. (I myself only gained authority in the last few weeks of my last term, and then only because my housemaster felt no boy should leave school without 'the experience of being a leader'.)

The big mistake of the system was its assumption that leadership is synonymous with the exercise of authority. In fact a good leader hardly needs to use authority at all. The qualities required are an ability to organise and communicate, consideration for other people, a vision of the future and an ability to convey a sense of shared purpose. It is highly desirable that some people should have all these qualities, but they are not necessary for everybody, and none of them is most effectively developed by the exercise of authority. If authority is merely delegated from someone further up the hierarchy, the qualities most likely to be acquired are assertiveness, complacency and ruthlessness.

To learn to lead, as opposed to command, children need to have examples to learn from and an opportunity to try. Such opportunities arise all the time in any school's social life. Someone has to organise a game, or an expedition, or a party, or a club, or a rock group. As soon as a small girl says 'Let's all go down to the copse' she is beginning to learn how to lead. She will learn better if her teacher, too, is a leader rather than an autocrat.

No one needs to be a leader all the time, and not everyone needs to be a leader at all, but the opportunity to test oneself out as a leader should be available. Too close a control of children by adults prevents this opportunity from arising.

7. Aesthetic values

A well-educated person is supposed to be able to appreciate Shakespeare and Beethoven and Leonardo da Vinci. (The enjoyment of the beauties of nature is supposed to come naturally.)

A far too frequent result of making appreciation of the arts a primary objective of education is that the pupils' eventual knowledge of the names everyone should appreciate is coupled with an inability to react sensitively to the art itself. I would like to call this intellectual snobbery, but it is not quite as bad as snobbery, because the names that are respected are truly deserving of respect; in this case it is just that many of the people paying respect do not understand the reasons for it. In short, children are too often taught what they ought to know without learning what they ought to learn. Musical appreciation does not spring, for instance, from the knowledge that Beethoven went deaf. Being able to list the important Italian Renaissance painters and their major works brings no one nearer to enjoying them.

The implication of a dictated list of great paintings is 'These are good. You must admire them.' Perhaps something can be learnt from such an approach – at least it should give the children a chance to see reproductions of the paintings – but a much surer way is just to show the children some pictures and say, 'I think these are marvellous. But see what *you* think of them.' This is to help develop taste rather than to teach people what is accepted.

But it is no good showing children paintings they don't like, playing them music they don't enjoy and insisting on all 16-year-olds studying *As You Like It*. You have to find works that are within their understanding, works that appeal to them. You must give children time. In aesthetic education discussion is important, but before discussion must come the lump in the throat or the shiver down the spine.

What we need to develop first in our children is sensitivity and taste. The knowledge is bound to follow, because they will wish to seek it out.

8. Development of individual talent
I suppose all schools want to develop pupils' talents. That's what music lessons, art lessons, woodwork and needlework are for.

The development of individual talent, though, means rather more than that. Each child will presumably need time for different things. Long stretches of time are needed – time for the children to write songs, or act, or make pottery or use whatever talents they have.

Anyone who has a talent is likely to want to develop it for the sheer pleasure of the thing. Compulsion and control are more likely to make children reluctant than to encourage them, however. All but the most single-minded, for instance, tend to give up learning musical instruments as soon as their parents will let them, because conventional music-teaching is so much a matter of drill rather than creativity.

What children need is first the opportunity to discover the talents they have, and secondly time to exercise them. During that time the teacher's role is to take the child's work seriously, to discuss, to offer ideas and to praise whatever is good. When a child persists in creative work without such support, it is to his or her credit rather than to the credit of the school.

9. Academic knowledge

People who send their children to independent schools rather than state schools often do so because they think the children will learn more. They are pleased if the children are worked harder and have more homework.

This raises two questions: First, is academic knowledge really so important; and secondly, if it is, is this the most effective way of achieving it?

It seems to me that no adult would think it important to learn a piece of information if he knew that, without making any particular use of it, he was soon going to forget it. That is what happens over and over again in schools. Children are deluged with information and obliged to attempt to learn it, after which, it is hoped, some few facts will remain with them.

What is the formula for compound interest? What is the chemical symbol for potassium? Who discovered the source of the Nile? Where did Alexander the Great die? The answers are important only if they interest you; if you are not interested it obviously does not matter whether you know them or not. If you are not interested it is also very much more difficult to learn.

I remember two occasions in my life when I was totally unable to memorise supposedly necessary information. One was when I was working with a firm that imported wine and I was supposed to learn the names of major French vineyards. I was not interested in the job, and I could not learn the lists. The other was when I arrived as a pupil at a new school and was expected to learn what the different colours on the caps meant. All my friends learnt them quickly, but I was at first uninterested and later resentful. In spite of being threatened with a caning if I failed to learn them, trying desperately and having special lessons with the matron, I never passed the test.

Almost all schools spend a great deal of effort in trying to force children to digest huge quantities of information about things that do not interest them. It would be far more sensible to start by helping them discover what they really want to learn. Then, instead of wasting their time in a depressing effort to memorise dull facts that they will probably soon forget, they could concentrate on the pleasure of learning things they will remember.

The irritating question of exams comes up here. Children may well need to pass exams in subjects that do not interest them. There is a simple way round this problem. Instead of saying, 'You must be entered for C.S.E. physics,' you say, 'If you want to get into the T.E.C. electronics engineering course you will have to get a grade 3 in C.S.E. physics,' and the child can accept it or reject it. Using this reasonable approach, progressive schools often have good exam results in even the most uninspiring subjects.

Too much information and too little understanding are a recipe for discouragement. A child who wishes to go to college or university must be prepared to pass the required exams. But beyond that, what is needed is not a memory crowded with facts and other people's opinions about them, but understanding and an enthusiasm for learning.

10. Social responsibility
Everybody will agree that children should grow up to be socially responsible. There is much less agreement over the question as to whether children can be socially responsible while still children. Some people believe that what you must do is make them *behave* responsibly by controlling them; others believe that you must make them *think* responsibly by allowing them freedom.

It seems plain to me that children who have always been carefully controlled will not know how to use freedom when

The admirable kind of self-confidence is confidence in oneself quite apart from membership of any group.

eventually allowed it. Children who have always been free will have had the opportunity to practise using their freedom in a comparatively protected environment. They will have had advice, time to make mistakes and time to learn. Social responsibility as an educational goal is therefore best reached at progressive schools.

11. *Self-confidence*
There are two kinds of self-confidence, one of which is admirable and the other deplorable.

The deplorable kind is self-confidence based on membership of a group. It is frequently a matter of social class. The public-school product will behave with arrogant ease in circumstances in which he should be sheltering in the background with becoming modesty. He does not mind making a fool of himself because he knows that his social status protects him and the old school tie brings tangible rewards. He would hate to admit it, but his bravado is very similar to that of any pushy young punk in a group of punks. His is not so much self-confidence as confidence in the protection of a superior group. Public schools deliberately foster this attitude.

The admirable kind of self-confidence is confidence in oneself quite apart from membership of any group. It is an understanding of one's worth, an awareness of one's own sense of values, an upright and realistic independence. It is not pushy or assertive, and it does not make itself conspicuous. It is a straightforward presentation of oneself as one really is.

Conventional schools may accept this independence of spirit when they find it or they may attempt to suppress it, but it is only the progressive schools that actively seek to foster it. At Risinghill Comprehensive School children who had been brought up to think very little of themselves were able to acquire proper self-esteem as a result of the school's progressive approach. In the wake of self-esteem came many other valuable qualities – among them openness, a sense of responsibility and even improved academic standards.

12. *A sense of purpose*
Conventional opinion usually interprets a sense of purpose as ambition. While I was at Repton the headmaster, who must have been a sailing man, ended a valedictory sermon with the

words 'You are about to start on the great race of life. Five, four, three, two, one, BANG!'

Presumably in his mind he saw all his pupils speeding enjoyably off across the water, and was not too bothered that only one of them could win. Ambition is of course a purpose of a kind, but it is likely to be a selfish one; unless the aim is most wisely and modestly chosen, it is also going to be unfulfilled, and to leave a middle-aged person with an uncomfortable void.

People who believe in progressive education give a very different meaning to the phrase 'sense of purpose'. A self-confident school-leaver from a progressive school will be looking for something useful to do and will expect to find it. She will be aware of what her particular abilities are, and as a rational altruist she will want to put them at the service of mankind. She will have been used to planning her own time and making her own decisions; she will have had practice in achieving her own objectives rather than in merely obeying instructions; she will not have had her personal initiative stifled.

Such a person will be an embodiment of purpose, because her purposes will arise from her own personality. She may well have ambitions, but they will not be her fundamental motivation.

13. Kindness

My list ends with two simple words. The first is 'kindness'.

A school whose ex-pupils were mostly unkind or unhappy would obviously be a bad one, but some people are suspicious of simple objectives such as kindness and happiness because of their very simplicity. They might prefer to use such terms as 'altruism' and 'psychological adjustment' because they are afraid of seeming naive.

Headmaster Michael Duane, complained the scornful inspector at Risinghill, esteemed cordiality among the major virtues. Perhaps he would have been similarly scornful about kindness. Yet kindness – altruism, being disposed to do good to others – is surely the ultimate virtue. 'Love thy neighbour as thyself,' said Christ, and the words are often repeated in school assemblies all over the country.

You cannot be instructed in a virtue. You can perhaps learn to recognise it and to discuss it; you may even learn to imitate it; but you cannot actually acquire it simply by attending lessons. Luckily, a psychologically healthy child actually wants to be kind, so lessons are not necessary. The conditions for developing kindness are the same as those required for psychological health – that is to say, security and love. Once this start has been made, all that is needed is opportunity, appreciation and example.

I need hardly point out that these things are seldom present in any great quantity in conventional schools. In place of security and love you may find anxiety and suspicion, and for examples of kindness you often have to look to fellow-pupils and cleaners rather than to the teaching staff. The reason why progressive-school teachers try to provide security and love is not in order to make children respond, but because it seems the only ethical way to behave.

Naturally, the children respond.

14. *Wisdom*

My second simple word is 'wisdom'. Of course we want our children to be wise. Yet no one ever seems to say so. We may say we want them to be clever, or knowledgeable, or open-minded, perceptive, aware, skilful or well qualified, but we dare not say we want them to be wise. Perhaps this is because we are afraid we are not wise ourselves.

Wisdom in the sense I mean is the ability to make good use of whatever knowledge one has; it is right judgement; it is true understanding. It cannot come from the mere accumulation of knowledge, but only from examination, discussion and questioning. It is not related to I.Q. or the amount of information you can memorise. It is more an attitude than an attribute.

The most important thing a school can possibly do is to give children this attitude.

School is not separate from life but part of it; development of the personality does not end when education ends. It is not what the children will have done by the time they leave school that matters, but their philosophy of life, both at school and afterwards.

We need to help children to understand their own individual importance so that they face the world with the friendly confidence that makes progress possible.

We need to help children to understand that it is a natural

human instinct to want to care for others, and that we suffer if we ignore this instinct.

We need to help children to understand what they themselves are capable of, so that they can use their talents to the full.

And we need to help children to understand that, as Euclid knew, learning is a pleasure. We do not want to learn primarily in order to gain higher status, or be better leaders, or earn our three-pence; we want to learn simply because we want to know.

Children who leave school understanding all these things will be wise – wise enough to understand also that their education is only beginning. All through their lives they will persist in the search for truth.

Questions parents often ask about progressive schools

Q. *What do you do about sex?*

A. Children are given information about the physical side of sex, including contraception, whenever it seems appropriate. As they reach adolescence and are increasingly in need of affection and support, they are encouraged to turn for advice to staff members, with whom they can discuss any question without fear of embarrassment or censure. As a result, their attitudes towards sex are generally quite sensible.

Sexual intercourse is illegal below the age of 16, but no school, no matter how strict, can control sexual mores by authority alone. It is not possible to supervise children all day and all night. The staff at a successful progressive school depend more on the values of the subculture than on rules.

Because the subculture is much closer to the surface than at a conventional school, the adults are more likely to be aware of its values. It is also more likely that teenagers will actively seek the opinions and experienced advice of adults who are able to reinforce the natural feeling that sex should not be exploitative, and that any sexual relationship should be a loving one. In any case the staff try to make sure that their opinions are known; children are strongly influenced by adults who like them and whom they like.

I have no statistics as to whether there is more heterosexual activity in a progressive school than homosexual activity in a single-sex school. Indeed it is hard to see how anyone could arrive at honest figures about such a private business. However, almost all children at progressive schools are exceptionally at ease with the opposite sex; in an atmosphere where mutual respect prevails they are able to show affection without sexual overtones.

I have heard of only 5 pregnancies among Dartington Hall pupils during my 25-odd years at the school.

Q. *What do you do about drugs?*
A. Drugs are another matter that can be effectively controlled only by the subculture. All sensible progressive schools have some strict rules about drugs; for instance, pupils may be sent home for a stated period the first time they are caught using drugs, and they may well be expelled if it happens again. However, as in any traditionally run school, the children's own attitudes are a more important influence than school rules.

A close and supportive relationship with an adult is likely to be a strong influence on any child. Progressive-school pupils are often encouraged to choose one member of staff as a tutor in the hope that the relationship will develop into a friendly and frank one. It is through such relationships that accurate information can be fed into the subculture, and open discussions of the problems of drug-taking can then take place without awkwardness. Just as violence from teachers tends to lead to violence in the subculture, so reasonableness tends to lead to reasonableness.

It is impossible for any school to prevent the use of cannabis. At a progressive school, however, the pupils are likely to be better informed, and their attitude more mature, than at institutions where staff and students keep at a distance from one another.

Q.· *Why don't you have compulsory religion?*
A. It is not possible to enforce religion. You can take a child to the altar, but you can't make him think. Children who want to go to church or synagogue should of course be free to do so. Information about religion should be readily available. But we try to avoid unbalanced and powerfully expressed moral pressure to join any particular group, whether it be the Church of England or the Communist Party.

Q. *What do you do about children who refuse to do what you tell them to?*
A. The first thing to do is to wonder whether the original demand was sensible; the child may well have a perfectly good

reason for rejecting it. To insist on blind obedience may sometimes make the teacher's life easier, but discussion and compromise have more educational value. Children react reasonably to reason. After all they come to school to learn, as well as to meet friends, talk and play. They expect the school to be organised in a way that enables them to do all these things.

Children, like adults, do have moments of rebellion or ill-temper when they disrupt the social atmosphere around them. If this happens too much, it is a sign, not of naughtiness which needs to be punished, but of disturbance that needs to be eased. In any such case the thing to do is talk, and to talk as sympathetically as possible. Understanding and affection are more effective than threats and anger.

Q. *What do you do about really disturbed children?*
A. Most progressive schools take a few children with behaviour problems because they can be more easily tolerated in a progressive atmosphere than elsewhere. Toleration alone is sometimes enough, and some problems disappear overnight. Others persist. The social atmosphere remains tolerant for quite a while, but not forever. When a school decides that the staff and other pupils cannot cope with a difficult child, one of two courses is possible: psychiatric advice may be sought, or the child's parents may be called in for a discussion, with the objective of finding some more suitable type of education.

Q. *What do you do about the three Rs?*
A. The three Rs are as important for a child at a progressive school as they are anywhere else. The style of teaching may be different but the objectives are the same. The best maths teachers everywhere believe that understanding should come before performance. With the other Rs the progressive view is that it is more important to be articulate than to be grammatical, and that it is principally through the *exercise* of language that a child learns correct usage. Language matures with maturity, and to insist on an adult style before it comes naturally is to inhibit the child's imagination and self-expression.

Most children learn to read by reading, and they learn to spell by writing. Those who fail to do so are given specific individual help.

Q. Since you don't have organised school teams, what do you do for children who are intensely competitive?
A. Progressive schools discourage competitiveness. To be over-competitive is as much a psychological problem as being timid or lazy. It is handled as other minor problems are handled: by being ignored. Extremely competitive children are treated exactly like the rest. Eventually either they gain in reasonable self-confidence and calm down or they continue to miss the competitive atmosphere and should probably be moved to a school where it is encouraged.

Q. Aren't progressive schools rather cut off from the real world, and therefore a poor preparation for it?
A. It is today's conventional schools, not the progressive ones, that deliberately cut themselves off. Prescribed uniforms, silence, no make-up, no pop-music, school bounds and so on are all attempts to keep the outside world away.

In a progressive school children are exposed to the discipline of reality rather than protected by a discipline of rules. This is the best possible preparation for the real future.

Q. My teen-age child doubts that she could trust herself with all this freedom. Is she right?
A. She may be. If she really fears freedom, she will probably be better off staying where she is. Perhaps she has been brought up to depend entirely on adult authority. If so, she may have difficulty learning to make her own decisions, or she may find it necessary to revolt as soon as she finds it possible. Adolescents like this can sometimes fail to fit into a progressive environment.

On the other hand, if she likes organising her own life and has a good relationship with adults she will probably cope with the freedom well.

A few facts about results

Exams in Perspective

A school's examination statistics are an inadequate way of measuring even the academic achievements within the school. They are affected by:

(1) the academic potential of the children admitted to the school in the first place.
(2) the school's concern for its own examination statistics (if you enter only children who you know will pass, you can expect a 100% pass rate).

Dartington takes children over a wide ability range and enters anyone who wants to sit an exam. It is also a small school, and its results fluctuate from year to year. The figures in the following table (for summer, 1983 – the most recent period for which full reports are available) give numbers of exams passed at Dartington in A-Level, O-Level and CSE. These are followed by percentages achieving the different grades, for comparison with national percentages from relevant exam boards.

There is little that can honestly be read from these figures except that at a good progressive school it is possible to do well in exams. Of that there can be no doubt.

A-Level	Total of passes	%A	%B	%C	%D	%E
Dartington	44	11	23	32	25	9
Oxford/Cambridge Board		19	24	24	19	14
London Board		13	21	20	22	24

O-Level	Total of passes	%A	%B	%C	%D	%E
Dartington	158	11	18	38	13	20
Oxford/Cambridge Board		19	28	34	9	10
London Board		13	26	35	11	15

CSE	Total of passes	%1	%2	%3	%4	%5
Dartington	122	24	15	24	28	9
South Western Board		14	23	26	24	13

Careers of A-Level Leavers

Of the 28 pupils who took one or more A-Level examinations in the 1982/83 academic year:

    3 chose to retake the exams to improve their grades.
    2 gained places in a diploma course in conservation crafts.
    2 are doing courses in art.
    1 is in secretarial training.
    1 is in training to become a State Registered Nurse.
    2 have jobs.
    2 went abroad for further study of languages.
   15 went on to degree courses, 13 of them at universities. The subjects they chose to specialize in: anthropology, architecture, art history, English, French and Italian, graphic design, landscape design, law, logic, mathematics, metallurgy, medicine, music, philosophy, Southeast Asian studies.

Where are the Old Girls and Boys?

Dartington does not keep formal records of ex-pupils. The following statistical breakdown of current careers is a very partial one, representing just over one-third of leavers – people the school has had recent news of – from the years 1971, '72 and '73:

Entertainment	8	Medicine	2
Teaching	7	Agriculture	1
Science	5	Air traffic control	1
Art and craft	4	Architecture	1
Social service	3	Estate management	1
University work	3	Film	1
Engineering	2	Music	1
Journalism	2	Nursing	1
Law	2	Public relations	1
Managerial work	2		

What the children say

The following verbatim comments from pupils currently at Dartington Hall's Middle and Upper Schools are a representative selection of reactions to the shift from conventional to progressive education. They are recorded here not because they are remarkable, but because they are typical of general attitudes.

* My old school used to split up boys and girls in games and things. When we were put in groups we were usually put girls in one, boys in another, and the Welsh children split up from the English ones. I didn't think about it much then but now it seems so much different and free. . . . All in all I prefer this place and I think it has changed me a lot.

* At my old school if you did something wrong they'd scream and shout at you so you were scared. Here they give you a quiet talking to and let you see the light. And the work is more fun. You learn just as much as you would in a comprehensive, if not more. In this school they give you help if you're dyslexic or not very good at maths. I'm very happy here. I've got lots of friends and you can really talk to the teachers like they're human, and in my other school they wouldn't listen to anyone – they're not human. Lots of people think this school is rubbish. I think they're wrong. At this school you *want* to work and go to lessons.

* The teachers here are very kind. They put themelves out or lose a bit of their free time to help you with your work. Dartington doesn't make you dying to do all the bad things

that there are to do, but it doesn't make you a goody-goody either. . . . At my old school people lied to get *me* in trouble instead of *themselves*, so I had to lie to get myself out of trouble, but at Dartington no one lies to the teachers. No one needs to.

* At my school before last the teachers treated me like some*thing* but not some*body*. Here they treat us as a person. Here they *ask* you to do something, while at my school before last I was *told* to do something.

* At my last school, if the teachers blamed me unfairly for something and I tried to stick up for myself they told me not to answer back, it was rude to. I couldn't talk openly to teachers as I can here. I think being able to call my teachers by their first name or a nickname is very good; it brings the relationship between teacher and pupil closer.

* At my primary school all the teachers were very superior to us. They were on one side and we were on the other. If we did anything wrong – usually it was very trivial such as breaking a mug or swearing – we had to stand outside the headmaster's office. It was opposite the staff room and when the teachers came out they all stared at us or made a stupid comment such as 'Naughty naughty' or 'What have you been up to then?' When I was about 6 I had to stand there crying all lunch break, because I had spilt some drawing pins on the floor and someone had told on me even though I had picked them all up.

* At my old school when we woke up I used to think, 'School today. Oh no!' Here you wake up and you think, 'School. I wonder what we're going to do today.'

* I'm very pleased that I came here because otherwise I would never have been doing well in anything, least of all music, but now I play and enjoy three instruments, and in two of them I am doing grade three in about two or three terms. . . . Also here you just walk out when you want to go to the toilet, but I used to have to ask whether you could go, and if they said 'No' you were in great trouble.

* When I first came here it was difficult to adjust and for me to become socially acceptable within the school. But I've grown up a lot and now I have adulthood looming in front of me. Relationships between friends were un-complex and emotional problems were hidden at my last school. Here, though, friends help you sort yourself and your life out. People aren't afraid of teen-age problems and to talk about them. At my age (17) you're changing physically and mentally. It's a difficult time. But here it's like having 10 brothers and 10 sisters all willing to help me out at any time. This may not be an important part of a progressive school to the outsider but to me it is. You may say that it can happen in every boarding school. But here – well, it's special. The atmosphere is right for healthy relationships.

* My last school was a convent which was very secluded and sheltered. It was work- and religion-orientated. You were put on one stern line, and if you moved off it you were out. When I came to Dartington my eyes were suddenly opened. I began to see life and see what friends were. . . . The convent made you scared of adults and think you were inferior. Adults here are much more on your level. My life has changed dramatically for the better.

The anti-progressive bias of the press

In 1983 the country's papers printed news items about problems in several independent schools. According to the papers, Eton expelled 1 boy and suspended 6 others for vandalising the parish church and trying to remove the organ pipes; Stowe sacked 12 and suspended 5 for drug usage after pupils had stolen a master's car to go to a party in the middle of the night; 5 cannabis-smokers were expelled from Fettes and 2 from Eton; 4 'suppliers' of cannabis and LSD were expelled from Repton; and a dead baby was found in a locker at Badminton. These reports may or may not be accurate, but they are certainly fairly sensational. Nevertheless, as far as I know, none of them was accorded more than half a column of space in any of the major national papers.

On the other hand, no one can have missed the extensive front-page coverage on Dartington Hall, a progressive school where the police did not make a single prosecution after a drugs raid. It was branded as a 'vice' school after the recently appointed headmaster, who was apparently shocked to find some social problems at the school (of a kind that anyone might expect at any school), wrote a letter to all Dartington parents in which those problems were grossly exaggerated. A copy of the letter found its way to the press and its contents became big news.

The media did not print front-page stories, however, about comments from the head of police in Totnes, Devon, where Dartington is located. How widely disseminated was his remark to the *Daily Telegraph* that the 'one or two problems' at Dartington made it no different from 'any other school on my patch'? How much space was allotted at the height of the crisis to an interview with the public relations officer of the Devon police in which he said, 'The charges are very minor – nothing of any consequence. . . . The police have got a perfectly good working relationship with the school; there are no specific problems over which there is any particular cause for concern; no problems that they don't have in any other school; this has all got out of proportion'?

Eventually it was reported that the head himself was not above reproach, and after only one term at Dartington he was forced to resign. For some obscure reason this also seemed to bring discredit on the school; his dubious past proved to be almost as damaging to its reputation as his dubious accusations.

Less than a year later, the name of Dartington Hall was once again unfairly blackened by the national press – this time with even less justification – when one of its pupils was drowned. Reports of the inquest stressed 'facts' that were either false or were more nearly innuendo than fact. It was reported that Cathy had drowned in a pool in the school grounds; that the school caretaker was somehow involved; that the boys who found her body were Dartington boys who had been taking drugs; and that one of the witnesses was in the habit of picking up girls in the school bar.

The actual facts: Cathy was drowned in the river Dart, which does not run through the school grounds. The caretaker worked for another school, not Dartington. The boys were not Dartington Hall boys. Dartington Hall School has no bar.

There was hardly any mention in the national press of Cathy's parents' expression of faith in the school and decision to continue to send her younger brother there. And only one paper – a local one – printed an interview with her grandfather in which he said, 'If this had happened at any other school, I do not feel the national press would have made such a fuss. My daughter, Cathy's mother, wants it to be known how happy she was at Dartington and how well she was looked after.'

If a boy at Eton vandalises the parish church, the papers do not blame Eton. When a girl at a girls' school becomes pregnant, the school is not held responsible. But to condemn a progressive school nothing as sensational as a vandalised church or dead baby is needed. As soon as there is some indication of normal adolescent misdemeanours or an accident occurs, it is seized on as proof of the general inadequacy of the progressive school's philosophy. The fact that most of the time the children are responsible and safe is overlooked.

The press reflects public opinion, of course, and there can be no doubt that the British public are prejudiced against progressive education. There are several possible reasons for this prejudice.

It may be that most people are inclined to believe, at least subconsciously, that nothing pleasant can do you any good, and the nastier a medicine tastes the better it is. In this view all pleasure corrupts, and the only way to virtue is through suffering. Progressive educators contradict this unhappy attitude, and for that reason their schools are harshly judged.

It may be, too, that some people mistakenly believe that the terms 'progressive' and 'permissive' are interchangeable, and at a progressive school there is always absolute permissiveness. (In fact, as I have shown in this book, even the most advanced of progressive schools find it necessary to place restraints on behaviour; the difference is that the children themselves are given the responsibility of deciding on the extent and nature of the restraints.)

A third reason for anti-progressive bias may be that adults who once had to struggle through a difficult educational journey for a dozen years, exhausting themselves and perhaps damaging their health, cannot look with equanimity at travellers who are coming an easy way, enjoying themselves thoroughly, and eager to travel further. How dare 'those despicable progressives' keep suggesting that though the journey is important, the unpleasantness is quite unnecessary?

But perhaps the most important reason for the opposition of the public (and the media that reflect public opinion) is this: progressive education, gentle and lacking in cutting edge though it is thought to be, nevertheless can be seen as a dangerous attack on the establishment. It has to be vigorously resisted. It has to be resisted for many of the very reasons that Christianity had to be resisted by the Romans. It rates truth above authority, persuasion above force, charity above conformity.

Conformity, force and authority have been questioned by moralists ever since moralists began asking questions, and the establishment has persecuted them. Perhaps the reason why so many people detest the progressive ideal is that its implications reach far beyond the walls of schools. If progressive methods are right, it may not be merely conventional education that is wrong, but also the basic structure of our society. Unwilling to face this possibility, people turn away uncomfortably; it is much less disquieting to read about the 'vice' at a progressive school than to risk doubting the generally accepted values of the world.

A list of interesting schools

When trying to choose a school for your children, always talk to the pupils as much as to the adults. Most school heads and teachers tend to be as misleading as their prospectuses when asked such questions as 'Do you cater for the needs of each individual child?' Don't rely on verbal replies. Look for the evidence. In a genuinely progressive school there is a spirit of mutual respect and consideration among teachers and children that becomes immediately evident to the alert observer.

Very few schools openly declare themselves for the type of education described in this book. Lists of educational institutions exist in abundance, but, to the best of my knowledge, there is no such thing as a selected list of schools that say they operate in accordance with progressive principles. The following list, therefore, comprises only a few schools here and abroad which have been recommended to me. They tend to have these practices in common: they are coeducational, have no religious instruction, discourage competition, encourage children to call staff members by their first names, and have no prizes, prefects or uniforms.

I should be happy to hear from any school that feels it ought to be included in any future listing. Because of space limitations, primary schools (a great many of whom have already adopted progressive practices) are not included in the list below.

UK
Independent schools

Dartington Hall School
Totnes, Devon, TQ9 6EB
(0803) 862567

Frensham Heights School
Rowledge, Farnham, Surrey GU10 4EA
(025 125) 2134

Kilquhanity House
Kirkcudbright, Castle Douglas, Scotland

King Alfred School
Manor Wood, North End Road, London,
NW11 7HY   (01) 455 9601   *(day school only)*

St Christopher School
Letchworth, Hertfordshire, SG6 3JZ
(04626) 79301

Sidcot School
Winscombe, Avon, BS25 1PD
(This is one of a number of Friends schools which have long adopted many of the ideas in the book, although they have some religious instruction. For more information write to The Friends School Joint Council, Friends House, Euston Road, London, NW1 2BJ)

Summerhill School
Leiston, Aldeburgh, Suffolk

State schools

Bosworth College
Leicester Lane, Desford, LE9 9JL

Countesthorpe College
Winchester Road, Countesthorpe,
Leicester, LE8 3PR

Thomas Estley Community College
Station Road, Broughton Astley,
Leicester, LE9 6PT

Wreake Valley College
Parkstone Road, Syston, Leicester,
LE7 8LY

Stantonbury Campus
Bridgewater Hall, Milton Keynes,
Buckinghamshire

The Sutton Centre
Nottinghamshire

Quintin Kynaston School
Marlborough Hill, London, NW8

EUROPEAN SCHOOLS
For information write to the Association
for Experimental Schools at:
**Internationale Zusammenarbeit Von
Experimental Schulen**
Oberstufen-Kolleg, Postach 86.40, D4800
Bielefeld 1, Deutschland

GERMANY

Laborschule der Universität Bielefeld
Universitätsstrasse, D-4800 Bielefeld

Odenwaldschule
6148 Heppenheim 4, Ober-Hambach, Nr
Frankfurt

Schule Birklehof (Hochschwarzwald)
7824 Hinterzarten

Urspringschule (Schwäbische Alb)
7933 Schelklingen 1

For further information on independent
schools write to:
Stiftung Deutsche Landerziehungsheime
6417 Hofbieber 6

SWITZERLAND

Ecole d'Humanité
CH-6082 Goldern-Hasliberg

FRANCE

Ecole La Source
11 Rue Ernest Renan, F-92190 Mendon-
Bellevue, Paris

L'Ecole Alsacienne
109 Rue Notre-Dame des Champs, 75006
Paris

DENMARK

Tvind School
6990-Ulfborg, Jutland

SPAIN

Escuela Juan de Garay
Valencia

Escuela Benlliure
Valencia

USA

Happy Valley School
Ojai, California

Colorado Rocky Mountain School
Carbondale, Colorado

Putney School
Putney, Vermont 05346

Picture credits and acknowledgements

All the photographs in this book were taken by Steve Hoare except for the following:

Page
2	John Bulmer/Camera Press
18 (top)	John Sturrock/Network
48 (both)	The Photo Source
55	Mike Abrahams/Network
76	Ikon Research
102	John Sturrock/Network

Picture research was by Angela Murphy.

Most of what I say in this book is based on my experiences over the past twenty-five years at Dartington Hall School, and so my first debt of gratitude is to all the children and staff from whom I learnt so much. I also owe a great deal to Jeni Smith, who introduced me to Countesthorpe and expounded its philosophy. Donald Berwick performed the miracle of producing order where there was none, and my wife read every word and helped me to rewrite and re-arrange. To all these, to the people who have encouraged me by enjoying and approving of what I was writing, and particularly to the many people whose words I have quoted, I should like to express my thanks.

D G